DISCOVER
what
MATTERS

Find Meaning, Hope, and Love
in a Success-Driven College Culture

ELIZABETH McCOLLOCH

ELIZABETH ANN
PRESS

This is a work of nonfiction. The events and conversations in this book have been set down to the best of the author's ability, although some names and details have been changed to protect the privacy of individuals.

Cover & interior design: KUHN Design Group | kuhndesigngroup.com
Cover image: Shutterstock
Author photograph: Irene Searles

First paperback edition April 2024

Library of Congress Control Number: 2024900116
ISBN 979-8-9898497-0-3 (paperback)
ISBN 979-8-9898497-1-0 (ebook)

Published in Palo Alto, California by Elizabeth Ann Press

www.elizabethmccolloch.com

For Mom, Dad, and Steven

*I am grateful for your unwavering support throughout
the creation of this book. Even more, I am grateful for
your love and compassion during the hardest season
of my life. How blessed I am to be loved by you.*

PRAISE FOR *DISCOVER WHAT MATTERS*

"College students today face a variety of challenges on many fronts, including a strong cultural pull toward careerism. In *Discover What Matters*, Elizabeth McColloch draws on her own experiences to bring readers a fresh perspective on college as a formative time that equips students for a life of engaging in community and pouring into others. I pray that readers of this insightful book find it to be a helpful resource as they navigate a crucial hinge moment in their lives."

—**D. Michael Lindsay**, President of Taylor University and author of *Hinge Moments: Making the Most of Life's Transitions*

"As you're wrestling with big questions about your identity, belonging, and purpose, Elizabeth skillfully helps you pin down life-giving answers of meaning, hope, and love. You don't need to journey through this season alone; let this fantastic book accompany you as you cultivate a fulfilling life and develop deep relationships."

—**Kara Powell, PhD**, Chief of Leadership Formation at Fuller Seminary and Executive Director of the Fuller Youth Institute

"Elizabeth's authenticity, depth, humility, and vulnerability are fully displayed in this book. Drawing from personal experiences and timeless wisdom, she offers genuine insights that resonate with readers. Each page is infused with wisdom and compassion, gently nudging readers to delve deeper into their hearts and minds. Whether navigating relationships or personal growth, this book equips students with the tools and mindset needed to thrive in every aspect of life. *Discover What Matters* is a companion for the soul and a must-read for students preparing for college, attending college, or preparing to graduate. For those decades removed from college, it provides a sense of nostalgia and allows them to reevaluate their relationships, their sense of purpose, and how they show up for their loved ones and communities. On these pages, your transformative journey to living a life of purpose begins."

—**Monetta Edwards**, Director of the Winston Center for Leadership and Ethics at Boston College

"What makes a college experience—and a life—rich with goodness and meaning? With gentle wisdom and sensitivity, Elizabeth McColloch offers practical guidance for young people navigating the noise and hustle of an achievement-focused culture. Her book is the voice of a treasured friend you want to keep close—the one who shares the stories that change you, make you better, and give you hope."

—**Jennifer J. Camp**, author of *The Uncovering*,
a book of poetry, and *Breathing Eden*

"Through my work with teens and young adults, I see firsthand young people throughout the US suffering from mental health problems, with many experiencing psychological distress, loneliness, and suicidal behavior. By sharing her own difficult stories during college, Elizabeth reminds readers they are not alone and offers practical advice for seeking support. I highly recommend this book to any college student or high school student who is heading to college."

—**Christy Pierce**, author of *Life-Line: Help in a Mental Health Crisis, Shut Up: Silence the Negative Thoughts Inside Your Head*, and *God is Whispering to You*

"In *Discover What Matters*, Elizabeth McColloch offers a thoughtful examination of the emotional landscape of students' college years. Through heartfelt personal stories, she provides valuable guidance about taking the college experience to a higher level. As a college counselor for the past 25 years, I wholeheartedly recommend this for students who are ready to dive deeply into ways they can grow, manage challenges—such as loneliness or mental health issues—and make the most of this important transitional time."

—**Michelle Podbelsek**, Director of College
Counseling Associates, Silicon Valley

"This book is a prayer. Elizabeth shares her experiences and lessons learned to help young people as they try to navigate life, haunting expectations, and the overall college experience. The wisdom shared is an investment in self-discovery and love. Read on and then pass it on to others."

—**Karen Kiefer**, Director of The Church in
the 21st Century Center at Boston College

CONTENTS

PART 1: DISCOVER MEANING

PART 2: DISCOVER HOPE

PART 3: DISCOVER LOVE

PREFACE

I graduated from college in the spring of 2021. After spending many years of my life working toward that moment, it was so different from what I had envisioned for myself.

During my senior year, I experienced anxiety and panic symptoms, which had detrimental effects on my physical health. Instead of searching for a job like most of my peers, I was focused on trying to consume enough nutrients, manage the pain, and find my breath. As a result of frequent sickness, I developed agoraphobia and struggled to travel far from home.

There I was—a college graduate living back at home with no job prospects. I felt untethered. The future I had spent so long planning suddenly crumbled before I had even gotten a chance to build it.

Yet, during that season of pain and loneliness, I began reflecting on the previous four years of my life. Although my time at college had ended, I felt like the stories I had lived and the lessons I had learned were far from over. I couldn't imagine turning the page from that chapter of my life without recording the moments that had shaped me.

So, I started writing. And slowly, the words I put on the page began to morph into a book that I wanted to share with others.

This book became so many things to me during that difficult time. It was a reason to wake up in the morning, a creative outlet, a source of joy amid disappointment, and a compass pointing me forward when I felt lost.

But above all, it was a labor of love.

I wrote this book for every student who desires a meaningful college experience beyond the traditional "pursuit of success." Not only did I feel this way myself, but I encountered so many students who also wrestled with this tension.

As a sophomore at Boston College (BC), I was a resident assistant (RA) in a freshman dorm. In my role, I lived alongside students who were adjusting to life at college. I listened to their questions, comforted them on hard days, and laughed with them in joyful moments.

It was these conversations—the ones that happened in late-night hallway chats and long strolls around campus—that defined my experience as an RA. I was honored to support other young adults as they began to discern what mattered most to them. And now, I get to do the same for you.

Before we begin, I want you to imagine we are sitting in my RA room. You are on my red couch, and I am sitting crisscross applesauce on the floor across from you. A jar of candy rests on the small table between us. I tell you that you are safe to share your questions and stories, fears and longings.

You lean forward and whisper a question as if it's a secret ...

"So, Elizabeth, what do you think college is all about?"

I look around the room for a moment—my eyes falling upon a photo collage of smiling faces; a row of mugs sitting on the windowsill, holding memories of my companionship to residents during late-night "deep talks"; quotes that remind me to live with purpose; and the door that countless students walked through hoping to be heard, to be known, to be loved. I turn to face you again, a smile slowly spreading across my face.

"Well, it's the same thing life is all about."

And then I whisper my favorite line from the film *About Time*: "For me, it was always going to be about love."[1]

A NOTE ON FAITH

While I will share anecdotes about faith-based experiences and quotes from spiritual writers, this is not primarily a Christian book. Because my faith in Jesus is so integral to my identity and values, I would like to share the intention behind this decision. As an RA, I had the privilege of serving residents from various faith backgrounds. My desire was for any person who walked onto my floor to feel loved and welcomed just as they are. The same is true for this book—it is accessible to college students regardless of their faith background. If you are a person of faith, I hope your faith will be enriched by the stories I share. And if you are not a person of faith, I pray you will walk away from this book excited to embark on a meaningful college journey.

INTRODUCTION

A year and a half after graduating, I listened to a podcast episode of *Everything Happens with Kate Bowler* called "When Success Isn't Success." Bowler spoke with Harvard professor Arthur Brooks, who teaches a popular class on happiness. They talked about his experience of pursuing success in the world of classical music, only to encounter the devastating moment when his talent waned. As a result, he was left with a life that could no longer be defined by the measurable achievements he had once found his worth in.

Brooks reflected on an important conversation he had with his wife in the wake of his loss. She reminded him that he is more than his musical talent, and she pointed to the relationships in his life that were much more significant. Contemplating this realization, he spoke these beautiful words: "In the end, the only thing that matters is the sum of the love in your life."[1]

To be honest, if I had listened to this podcast as a high school student, I probably would not have believed him. I grew up in Silicon Valley, a place synonymous with innovation and achievement. Through middle school and high school, I felt immense pressure to live up to unrealistic standards of success that were embedded in the

culture around me. I sacrificed sleep, crammed my schedule, compared my academic performance with my peers, and never felt like I
was doing enough to reach the lofty goals I set for myself. At times,
that pressure felt suffocating.

Maybe you can relate. Maybe you know what it's like to try to
live up to these societal and personal standards at the cost of your
health, meaningful relationships, and authentic expressions of creativity. Maybe you feel exhausted by this way of life, but you can't
see an alternative path.

While there are many repercussions of our culture's obsession
with academic and professional accomplishments, there is one that
seems the most consequential: **The rewards of success and achievement are not strong enough to hold us up under the weight of really
heavy things.** Things like depression, loss, a broken heart, loneliness,
and illness.

During my time in college, I experienced some of these heavy
things. And when the pain was at its worst, I realized that it didn't
matter how many tests I aced or how polished my resume looked.
The superficial places where I searched for fulfillment brought no sol-
ace in the face of adversity.

There is certainly nothing wrong with having big dreams. In fact,
I hope this book will inspire you to pursue your goals with excitement and confidence. But when we become so fixated on external
measures of success, we lose sight of what really matters in life.

What we need when—in Bowler's words, "life comes apart"—is
meaning, hope, and love.[2] These things have sturdy legs. These things
will catch us no matter how far we fall, how many times we break,
and how distant we feel from the life we once lived.

Meaning that is uncovered in the beauty of the present moment.

That looks a lot more like opening ourselves up to the remarkable gifts that our ordinary lives hold instead of fixating on a future version of happiness that is always out of reach.

Hope to move us through painful seasons of our lives when we could easily let circumstances overwhelm us or push us into despair.

And *love* to draw us closer to the people who are right in front of us—people who we so often forget to appreciate in this increasingly disconnected world. It is this love that makes life so unbelievably beautiful, even as we grow older and awaken to the reality of just how heartbreaking life can be.

Maybe you can remember a time in your life when your days felt meaningful, when you looked to the future with hope, and when love was the bedrock that you built your life upon. Maybe you used to embrace life with a sense of wonder, but now you feel tired and burned out. Or maybe you are simply searching for encouragement from someone who has walked the college path and learned a thing or two about making these days count.

In the world around us, there are so many shiny objects, loud voices, and distracting screens that pull at our attention. Amid this craziness, the important parts of life often fade into the background. My hope is that this book will act as a lantern, illuminating what we have lost or neglected along the way. And as you read, may you awaken your appreciation for life and ignite your passion for learning. May you renew your hope for a brighter future. May you uncover the beauty of authentic relationships as you lay down the heavy weight of judgment, both toward yourself and others.

And just maybe, you will see that college is an opportunity to discover what matters most.

PART 1

DISCOVER MEANING

THE BEAUTIFUL IS CLOSER THAN YOU THINK

During the first week of college, I attended my school's freshman convocation, a ceremony to honor the beginning of our college journey. We dressed up in pretty dresses and fancy suits and proceeded together down Linden Lane. On that day, we walked as one.

However, as our journey continued, each of us had to learn to forge our own path. This might sound scary, but I think it can be exciting. Instead of getting caught up in our culture's view of a "meaningful college experience," how might we as individuals move closer to purpose, beauty, and joy?

Take a moment to reflect on this question: *What would a meaningful college experience look like for me?*

Don't be surprised if your answer changes over the course of your college adventure. I know that my answer certainly changed. For many years, I thought that college would be a stepping stone to a meaningful future. But over time, I came to see that we don't work our way toward meaning, at least not in the traditional sense.

As you read Part 1, I will ask you to reexamine your perception of a meaningful life. What if fulfillment doesn't come from achieving outward success but from experiencing internal transformation? What if we can savor our ordinary lives instead of wishing for flashier ones? What if we can devote ourselves to activities because they fill us with an authentic sense of purpose, not just because they appear noteworthy? What if meaning is not some elusive, far-away thing available only to people whose lives look perfect on paper?

What if the beautiful is actually closer than we think? Wouldn't that be something?

CHAPTER 1

THE PERFECT
SNOW DAY

On Cultivating Meaningful Moments

*The world will never starve for want of
wonders; but only for want of wonder.*

G. K. CHESTERTON[1]

Dear resident,

I still remember the giddiness I felt on that chilly December day of my first Boston winter. Sitting in a small lecture hall, I tried to concentrate on the final presentations in my Science and Technology class. But the sight of something beautiful outside the window tugged at my attention. I found myself sneaking frequent peeks at the steady flutter of snowflakes dropping from the sky and lightly coating the benches in the small alcove beside our classroom.

When we entered the classroom that morning, the snow was just beginning to fall. Instead of sticking to the ground, it had melted into small puddles. But as we emerged from hours inside, a little drowsy from sitting through so many presentations, we saw that a beautiful, thick coat of snow had blanketed our campus. And the falling flakes showed no signs of stopping anytime soon.

I ambled around with three fellow Californians as we reveled in the magical feeling of seeing a campus we loved transform. A vast whiteness enveloped the sky as far as the eye could see. Snow piled up on benches and settled like small hats on the black lanterns lining the million-dollar stairs. We saw that our campus, with its magnificent Gothic-style buildings adorned with green-tiled roofs and stone siding, had been missing its winter wardrobe. Now, at last, the bride had found her perfect white dress.

Several hours later, my friends and I stood in our bathing suits in the freezing evening air. We lined up near the entrance to our dorm underneath trees that wore snow like crystal jewels. Then we began counting down: "Three, two, one"—and before you could say "hypothermia," we threw off our coats, fell back into the snow, and flailed our arms and legs frantically while shouting with equal parts glee and discomfort. The adrenaline coursing through my body protected me from the worst of the bitter cold as my bare skin sank into the snow. A few seconds later, we all jumped back up and found refuge in our warm coats. When I look back at my journal entry from that night, appropriately titled "A Magical Day," I smile as I read the words I scribbled with excitement: "This was definitely one of the best days of my life."

With delight and wonder,
Elizabeth

Redefining meaningful moments

Before college, I had an idealistic vision for my life—one that was memorable, impactful, and appeared significant. I set my sights on bold ambitions like becoming an influential entrepreneur or a distinguished writer. I thought that my life would matter only if I left a visible mark on the world. And so, I often dismissed ordinary days as insignificant, instead looking ahead to future moments when I would finally live out my ambitions.

This mindset also led me to approach many moments in life as a performance. Whether I was hosting a casual game night or going to prom, I couldn't help but wonder what other people thought of me. With the rise of social media, it is tempting to try to orchestrate experiences that others will deem interesting. If you have felt this way, you are not alone. However, our lives are meant to be lived, not just curated for admiration.

As I recall the experiences that helped me redefine "meaningful moments," that cold December day comes to mind. Though I spent many days focusing on how others perceived me, on that day, I got lost in the beauty of my surroundings. I was captivated by the enchantment of the season's arrival and swept up in the excitement of novel adventures. Just as the snow helped me to see my campus in a new light, this experience woke me up to the marvels that my ordinary life could hold.

Perhaps it was the fast-moving pace of college life, but something deep inside me knew that those days would not last forever. I needed to notice significant moments when they came—and savor them. And just maybe, those moments would reveal my capacity for amazement, which I thought was lost long ago.

As I continued my college journey, I realized that our most memorable experiences often won't be the ones in which we achieve some impressive feat or reach some important milestone. **In fact, it is not the exterior appearance of moments in our lives that makes them significant. Rather, it is the way we pay attention to and savor these moments that gives them meaning.**

Cultivating meaningful moments in our everyday lives

As I recall my college days, it is easy to feel nostalgic for the many memories that come to mind. But sometimes, it is hard to identify the special quality of these moments when we are right in the middle of them. Not every moment will glimmer like the sun on a fresh blanket of snow. When we are waking up to an ordinary day and living our ordinary lives, we forget that one day we may look back on the routines, encounters, and simple delights unique to that season with a particular fondness. And so, I would love to share how I created space to cultivate those meaningful moments at college.

While some of those moments were solitary, many of them involved people I love. When life gets busy, I am tempted to rush through my day independently, forgetting to bring others along with me. But in doing so, I miss out on the gift of shared experiences. Not only do shared experiences add a spirit of joy and a sense of connectedness to our lives, but they also strengthen the friendships we are forming. And so, I encourage you to invite others into the spontaneous adventures of your everyday life.

I remember with fondness simple activities that were far more enjoyable when I involved friends in them. Whether we were cooking breakfast together, washing my roommate's car at the local car wash, or grabbing groceries, being with my friends reminded me that I wasn't alone in the human experience. And these simple activities often created space for more serious conversations to arise organically—a benefit I certainly enjoyed due to my unabashed affection for "deep convos."

Many of the moments I cherished also had a feeling of novelty to them. I read an article about a young woman who tried to do one new thing each day when she was struggling with anxiety and depression.[2] While the experiment was incredibly effective at improving her mood, it can also be helpful for those who have found themselves stuck in routines that feel mundane.

I didn't have to go far to find something new to experience. Studying in new coffee shops, trying my first apple cider donut one New England fall, and taking a Zumba class are just a few memories that come to mind. Experiencing simple pleasures for the first time reminds us that the delights we have already tasted still have something sweet in them worth savoring. If your routines and responsibilities are dragging you down, consider trying something new, even if it is small. A fresh spark can awaken us to the delights of our lives when our outlook has become stale.

Finally, some of my favorite moments involved a bit of silliness and creativity. I recall decorating my door with my roommates by fashioning fence posts out of cardboard pizza boxes, baptizing one

friend in a fountain on a cold night, and taking part in an event-
ful scavenger hunt through Quincy Market. I think it was the very
unconventional nature of these experiences that gave them their
memorable quality.

One of Mary Oliver's most famous lines of poetry reads, "Tell
me, what is it you plan to do with your one wild and precious
life?"[3] Oliver's call to live a *wild life* does not strike me as an appeal
to act recklessly but rather as a caution against exalting comfort,
ease, and the accomplishment of our well-laid plans as the ultimate measures of a good life. Moreover, when we see our lives as
precious, we realize that the value of a day is not determined by our
wavering feelings toward it, but by the unshakable gift of waking
up in it. This is a gift we certainly do not want to squander by living half-heartedly.

Instead of going through the motions of my life, I want to greet
each new day with a spirit of enthusiasm. What about you? What
would it look like for you to imbue typically tedious experiences with
your unique creative imagination?

As you look at the calendar, your week may be filled with long
study sessions, an eye doctor appointment, and several practices for
that sports game or theatrical performance you are nervous about.
But what about that gap on a Thursday evening? Could you call up
a few friends to work on a creative project just for the sake of spreading joy? Could you create a decorative display to brighten up your
dorm's bland hallway, write a song together, or assemble candy bags
for unsuspecting students in the library? When you look back on
these days, can you imagine that you will regret carving out time to
remind yourself what a wonder it is to wake up, yet again, in a world
that can still astonish you?

Savoring the sacred in the ordinary

A few years ago, I discovered a ministry called "Sacred Ordinary Days," which creates spiritual formation resources.[4] When I read their name, I immediately fell in love with the term. As I look back on my college journey, I know I got a glimpse of the sacred moments nestled into my "ordinary life."

An important part of savoring the sacred in our ordinary days is taking the time to slow down, look up, and notice what is around us. So often, we are setting our sights on the upcoming event on our schedule or the next item on our to-do list that we forget to delight in the present moment. *Noticing* looks different for each of us. Perhaps for you, it means naming what is beautiful out loud. Perhaps it means taking a photo. For me, noticing happened in one-second increments.

At the end of my senior year of high school, my brother introduced me to an app called "1 Second Everyday Diary."[5] The concept is simple: You take a one-second video each day and plug it into the app, which compiles the clips into a collection. Then, you can view this video diary and fondly reflect on a particular period of your life, depending on the time interval you choose. I still have the app, but I used it most faithfully during my freshman year of college.

My new friends soon became accustomed to me pulling out my phone at random times to record a second-long video. And while some videos show birthdays and milestone moments, most clips capture perfectly ordinary occasions. We drank cups and cups of tea; savored cheesy, delicious flatbread pizzas; and cheered enthusiastically at ice hockey games. I balanced water bottles and books on my head for my friends' entertainment, drew graphs on chalkboards in late-night study sessions, and worked in the serenity of the library as bookshelves swallowed me up. The app was a reminder that every-day moments are worthy of recognition. Because in the end, these are what comprised my college journey—beautiful, silly, mundane, exhilarating ordinary moments.

What about you? If you were to record a one-second video each day, which instances would you capture? What are the ordinary moments you wouldn't want to forget? What are the uniquely ridiculous patterns you have developed, the inside jokes you have shared with your friends, and the tiny glimpses of heaven you have encountered on your early evening walks? As you begin to answer these questions, you might just find that these ordinary moments belong to a greater web of people, places, and experiences that make up your life—a life that is undeniably sacred.

When wonder feels far away

Yet, what about the days that feel far from wonder-filled? Like when you sacrificed sleep for yet another impossibly rigorous midterm and are walking like a zombie to class the next morning. Or when your weekend plans are not glamorous or enriching—and instead look a lot more like doing three hours of laundry, walking to the grocery store on a frigid day, and calling a customer service agent for help with your phone bill (which entails a lot of that dreaded elevator music on repeat). Or the days when you feel a sense of loneliness emerge, and you fear you are missing out on the "amazing college experience" that everyone else appears to attain with ease. I will address some of these more disappointing moments in our college experience in Part 2. But for now, I would like to invite you to view these days simply as opportunities to pay attention.

What does it look like to pay attention? In the age of social media and instant entertainment, our collective capacity to exercise this muscle has diminished. But I think we can grow adept at this skill once again. I have found that paying attention does not need to require looking out for large wonders or disruptions in my day. Maybe it means strolling down a street I have walked 100 times and discovering something I had never noticed before. Or it could look like calling the grocery clerk by name and being in tune with her emotions rather than staring at my hands while she bags my food.

Oftentimes, when we set an intention to try something new, we cling to it with fervor. But this posture of paying attention looks more like letting go of something. We must release our grip on the present and our desire to control the future. We must choose to see what is right in front of us without letting our mind wander to more "important tasks" or replaying moments from our day. Paying attention is one of those practices that is simpler than we imagine and yet often far more difficult than we would like it to be.

In a beautiful ode to the value of paying attention, Anne Lamott shares this reflection in her book *Bird by Bird: Some Instructions on Writing and Life*: "There is ecstasy in paying attention...Anyone who wants to can be surprised by the beauty or pain of the natural world, of the human mind and heart, and can try to capture just that—the details, the nuance, what is. If you start to look around, you will start to see."[6]

Lamott is speaking not only to writers but to anyone who wants to be more attentive to the world around them. She is calling us to be "observers," whether we are doing our laundry, walking to the bus stop, or wandering through the aisles of the grocery store. I want to be awake to the world around me. I want to see who and what is in front of me. And I want to remember that each day—though it may look the same on the surface—holds unique treasures that distinguish it from the last.

So, when you don't feel particularly captivated by the world around you, perhaps you can shift your goal to paying attention. This may open the door to opportunities for delight that were hidden before, ultimately leading to one of those meaningful moments I described earlier. Or perhaps you will simply gain a broader perspective on a place, a person, or a routine than you began the day with.

It can be humbling to adopt the posture of paying attention as we learn to become observers. In doing so, we step back from our place at the center of our lives. Contrary to how this may seem, sometimes this is the very best thing we can do. There is freedom in not always trying to fix our circumstances or find meaning in every moment. As patient observers, we are witnessing life unfold before us in both expected and unexpected ways. And we are learning to be present for it. Maybe this is enough when wonder feels far away.

Remnants of wonder

Somewhere between the days when wonder feels far away and the many moments that we are learning to savor for their ordinary beauty, there may be a few moments that carry a supreme significance in your mind. These moments glimmer in your trove of memories. They hold a vibrancy that is only visible every once in a while—when the light shines just right or that song hits the perfect note, vibrating outward in an endless echo.

I recently rewatched the coming-of-age film *The Perks of Being a Wallflower*. In the last scene, the characters drive through a tunnel listening to music with the windows down. As we see the protagonist Charlie standing in the back of a pickup truck with the wind rushing around him, we hear his voiceover with these words: "And in that moment, I swear we were infinite."[7]

Though some may regard this scene as cheesy, the sentiment behind Charlie's words resonates deep within me. As I recall these moments in my college journey, the ones that became memories I will forever carry with me, Charlie's words return to my mind. When I found myself lost in those experiences, I tried to pause and soak them in. I felt in my bones that these moments were transcendent—and now I think I understand his words more than when I first watched the film in high school. Because when you find yourself in a moment like this, you don't remember the past or worry about the future. You are just *right here* in the present, almost oblivious to the passing of time.

The way the frozen snow felt underneath my bare back as I laughed with delight. The peace that overwhelmed me as I sat on a small rock watching the most brilliant orange sunset over the reservoir, the silhouette of Gasson Hall stretched gloriously in the background. Sitting around a bonfire by the lake at a retreat as we roasted marshmallows and talked long into the night. The fresh air filling my lungs as I ran up Common-wealth Avenue past bakeries and Tudor-style houses and Bostonians who made me feel like I was starting to belong there. Laughing as two of my best friends, Will and Nick, rapped the words to a song I didn't know— but it didn't matter because I was with them and we were moving fast through the night.

I hope you will let your experiences like these grow a sense of wonder in you for the world you live in and the people who are a part of your story. Lean into these moments, however fleeting they may be, and notice how you feel in your bones. Take some time to reflect: *Do you feel grateful? Do you feel fully alive?* Perhaps you feel like a long-ing in you has subsided just a little, the way the ocean washes up to the shore and then slowly recedes, only to reveal what was beautiful in the glistening sand all along.

The beauty of these wonder-filled moments is that they leave something behind for us long after they have passed. They remind us of what matters to us (and also how much is insignificant). They show us that we are capable of being touched by beauty—and forever changed. They remind us that even though life can sometimes be hard and other times dull and mundane, we can still experience delight in the folds of our everyday lives. It is this realization that draws us closer to the life of meaning we all crave. And it gives us a newfound peace with our lives as they are, not as we wish they were.

Sometimes, we can plan these moments, but often they come to us as gifts. So, when you receive these special presents, here's my invitation to you: Practice sitting in the moment without worrying when it will end. Tell the people you are with that you love them. And reflect on this moment far into the future so it will become an ingrained memory that shapes the person you are becoming.

After the moment has passed, continue to search for beauty again and again. If you are struggling to find it, may you derive inspiration from the words of Cheryl Strayed's late mother, which are captured in the film *Wild*: "There is a sunrise and a sunset every day, and you can choose to be there for it. You can put yourself in the way of beauty."[8]

May we all seek to live this way—to show up where we know we will find beauty. Maybe we will walk the long way home so we can pass the brick house on the corner that reminds us of a fairy-tale cottage. Maybe we will leave the library once the sun has set so we can see the trees lit up against the backdrop of the dark, velvety winter sky. Maybe we will poke our heads out of a book in the dining hall when we hear a friend calling our name so we can see their radiant smile cast just for us. Or maybe we will wander our beloved campus with its newly bestowed wardrobe, amazed that we get to call this place home. In doing so, may we remember that the beautiful just might be closer than we think.

CHAPTER 2

SUNDAY NIGHTS ON FLOOR ONE

On Conversations That Matter

Dear resident,

I remember the nervous anticipation that arose in me as I sat in the Loyola One lounge on an April evening of my sophomore year. This lounge had been the site of countless study nights, a Thanksgiving weekend horror movie marathon, and a few dance parties when we were too tired to complete yet another problem set. But that night, the lounge had a different purpose.

I could see students walking down the hall, past glass walls that created a fishbowl effect. Every so often, someone would stop in front of the door and pull on the surprisingly heavy handle to enter the room. As people began to fill up the couches and chairs I had arranged in an oval, the pounding in my chest became louder. I suppose it was alerting me that something important was starting.

Although that lounge was not my home, I still believed I could extend hospitality to my guests. As I excitedly welcomed new and old friends into the space, I hoped they could sense the love and grace that were already present in our new community.

Once people had settled in, I shared a vision for the group: over the next five weeks, we would gather to discuss Bob Goff's book *Everybody, Always*.[1] This book, as well as Goff's first book *Love Does*, inspired me to pursue meaningful relationships, especially with people who had different life experiences than me.

After expressing my excitement, I clicked play on the introduction video that would begin each session. A smile stretched across my lips as I heard laughter spreading behind me in response to Goff's signature humor. When the video had finished, we sat in small clusters on the floor, sharing our responses to several small group discussion questions. I appreciated the honesty that people brought to the groups. We spoke about how Goff's words inspired us to expand the circle of individuals we interacted with. And we mentioned specific people in our lives who we wanted to show more grace to.

Over the course of five weeks, several students gathered in the lounge every Sunday night. As we sat together, we offered comfort, wisdom, and encouragement to one another. And we learned how to *just listen*—a sacred practice that has become a lost art on many college campuses.

A few days after the final *Everybody, Always* gathering, I walked up to my door to find a pot of beautiful pink hydrangeas with a card signed by members of the community we had formed in the Loyola One lounge. When I opened the card, I read heartfelt words of gratitude from these dear friends. I was immediately overwhelmed by their thoughtfulness. Reading the many names on that card, I realized with amazement that our time together each Sunday night left a significant impression not only on my life but on their lives too.

With gratitude,
Elizabeth

Conversations that change us

I share this story with you because it challenged my initial perception of conversations that "matter" on our college journey. Throughout my four years, I was a part of many organizations and campus groups. While I enjoyed these communities, I admit that part of my motivation for joining them was the feeling of importance they gave me. I viewed my participation in these groups and the leadership positions I held as "measurable markers of success."

I understand the belief that conversations most important for our growth and development must happen in formal classroom settings or club meetings. But when I led that small group, I realized just how significant informal experiences can be too. **I am learning that important conversations do not matter because they are "measurable." Rather, they are significant because they change us.** And isn't that the point of college? Don't we want to walk away transformed?

The value of time

As I ask myself why it can be so hard for us to believe that these conversations are worth making time for, the concept of "value" comes to mind. If we have many responsibilities and roles in college, it can be difficult to determine how to prioritize our time. It can be easy to deem certain activities more "worthwhile" than others based on their potential to push us up an invisible ladder of success.

I know what it is like to walk around with this deep-seated fear that I am wasting important days on pursuits that will not have a long-lasting impact. This fear manifested in my tendency to seek out clubs and projects I could invest time in because I thought they would satisfy my longing to live a life of impact. But this approach had its drawbacks. If we only say yes to opportunities because they appear significant on paper, we might miss out on the experiences we long for deep down.

In her beautiful book *Growing Slow*, Jennifer Dukes Lee says, "Time is not a commodity to be used but a gem to be treasured."[2] Her words challenge my instinctive transactional view of time and my narrow mindset around "what has value." In order to treasure the time I have, I want to fill it with conversations that are life-giving, not just ones that appear significant from the outside. Many of the conversations that I cherished in college felt valuable because they allowed me to connect with the people I loved. Often, this happened in ordinary ways. Memories like late-night talks on the floor of our dorm hallway, spontaneous chats in the communal bathroom, and stories shared over retreat campfires come to mind.

Why we showed up

"The *Everybody, Always* group," as we came to call it, differed from many of the "traditional" communities I was a part of in college. This informal group was not connected to a club or campus ministry organization. Nobody took attendance or gave us credit for our participation. This meant that we showed up because we believed in the message of Goff's book and the power of community to help us live the message out in courageous ways.

Looking back, I am thankful that the group members showed up as their authentic selves. In the college environment, we so often try to craft eloquent arguments to garner admiration, dress a certain way to earn acceptance, and surround ourselves with people who admire our achievements. But on Sunday nights in the Loyola One lounge, we had the freedom to show up just as we were. We came as our tired, imperfect selves seeking—as the Catholic Peace Prayer says—"to understand more than to be understood."[3]

This group felt like a sacred opportunity to show up each week to have conversations that mattered. We spoke about our longing to love more wholeheartedly and to show compassion when apathy was far easier. We came for community, for connection, and for an hour of peace and laughter amid our stress-filled weeks. We came because we believed that the people we are in private matter just as much as the ones we are in public. And we came because deep down, we knew that the way we love is far more important than the accolades we collect.

In the rest of this chapter, I will share some lessons that I learned from the *Everybody, Always* group and a popular campus event that expanded my view of conversations that matter. As you read, ask yourself what spaces you can walk into during this next season of your life. Perhaps this looks like joining a small group that meets at a consistent time. Or maybe it looks more like sitting with a few friends in your hallway to reflect on the sweet moments from your week and the harder ones that left you feeling uncomfortable and disappointed. Wherever these conversations take place, may you show up with courage. And may you experience their power to draw you closer to others while also inviting you into deeper places of self-reflection.

Don't be afraid to go deep

When we gather together, we discover just how much we can relate to one another. Sometimes, we forget how much we have in common with the people we sit across from—in ways that may be hidden at first. In college, we often find "our people" as we connect over obvious similarities. Maybe we share the same major and enjoy talking about our career ambitions. Or perhaps we bond over our enjoyment of tailgating at football games. These connections can be very enriching. But we can also connect on deeper levels as we have honest conversations that pull us from our feelings of isolation.

In this small group, I realized that the people I often viewed as "easygoing" or "loving" were more multifaceted than I had initially believed. It surprised me to learn that they also struggled to love the people in their lives who were not easy to get along with. *Could it be possible that we all wrestle with this discrepancy between our longing to love others wholeheartedly and the very imperfect ways that we treat each other?*

There is something about these realizations that make the college journey—and this human journey—a little less lonely. It might be easier to bond over our favorite musician or our obsession with iced mocha lattes. But learning how to relate to each other's weaknesses is an invaluable practice that we can carry with us into the rest of our lives.

While these meaningful exchanges may sound wonderful on paper, they do require a level of vulnerability that takes some getting used to. Try to walk into these conversations with an open mind, being patient with yourself as you discover what it looks like to show up authentically. It may take many conversations before you are comfortable connecting with friends on this level, and that's okay. Good things take time.

Adopt a listening posture

I still remember my first Socratic Seminar in eighth grade. I sat in a circle with half of my classmates, while the other half surrounded us in a larger circle. Their job was to track our participation, taking note of each time we spoke. Talk about pressure.

While the seminar was supposed to foster a thoughtful exchange of ideas, I was so focused on trying to interject my opinion that I hardly paid attention to the words my classmates were saying. Sure, I could hear sounds coming out of their mouths, but I was not truly listening.

I found that this trend continued in many of my college classes. While the environment wasn't as extreme as that middle school classroom, I did feel pressured to offer valuable insights. It appeared that students were commended for the words they spoke far more than they were for the intentional listening they exhibited. Perhaps that's because it is much easier to measure the contributions of a confident talker than the quiet value of a respectful listener.

And yet, listening is vital to having conversations that matter. The more we learn to listen with a receptive posture, the more we grow in humility. We realize that our voice, while important, is not the only voice worthy of being heard. And maybe our perspective is just one among many.

I discovered the importance of adopting a listening posture when I had conversations about faith in college. Within our *Everybody, Always* group, there were people from different faith backgrounds. Rather than distancing myself from friends who expressed their love for God in unfamiliar ways, I asked them to teach me about their practices and traditions. As I listened with the intent of learning, I admired their unique expressions of faith. And I carefully considered their responses before I shared my own views.

In college and society at large, we have become increasingly combative toward people with different beliefs. We hold on to our convictions so tightly that we leave little room for respectful dialogue. Yet, as I continued to have more faith-based conversations with my peers, I realized how much more we gain when we loosen our grip on the need to prove our point. In my experience, instead of separating us, acknowledging our differences and gathering together anyway emphasized everything that we *did* share. Most predominantly, we shared a deep desire to experience the beautiful mystery of God's love and share it with the people we encountered.

Agape Latte

Conversations that matter also pull us out of our narrow perspectives for a while and encourage us to keep the bigger picture in mind. Another experience that shaped my perspective on meaningful conversations was a "faith storytelling series" that BC's campus ministry hosted every month called Agape Latte. On one Tuesday night each month, students gathered in a campus café called Hillside. These evening conversations attracted students from various backgrounds, belief systems, and areas of study. We sat at tables scattered around the café, catching up with friends or grabbing treats while pleasant music played in the background. When it was time to begin, a speaker walked to the front of the room and shared their story with us.

I love the name that was chosen for this speaker series. According to the *Encyclopaedia Britannica*, *agape* refers to "the fatherly love of God for humans, as well as the human reciprocal love for God ..."[4] And *latte* refers to the coffee that the event's hosts served students. This combination of words reminds me of how often the deeply meaningful and the ordinary, practical parts of our lives intersect. These are the moments when we experience the *intangible* and *tangible* simultaneously.

As I recall these memorable evenings, a few specific speakers come to mind. I remember listening in amazement to Erik Weihenmayer, a BC alumnus and cofounder of an organization called No Barriers.[5] Weihenmayer shared his incredible story of summitting Mount Everest and kayaking through the Grand Canyon as a blind person. On Valentine's Day, I listened with joy as Ms. Smiley, the exuberant manager of a student support program at BC, shared her and her husband's beautiful love story with us.

Each speaker's story was unique. Some reminded us of our capacity to display great courage. Some entertained us with self-deprecating humor. And some made us cry as they showed us that hope is still available even in seasons of loss and heartbreak. But they all shared this special quality of leaving us with a deeper sense of possibility than we began the evening with. And their honesty invited us to be honest with ourselves about the values we want to live out.

Make space for reflection

So, how do we make space for conversations that matter and the internal reflection that comes along with them? As you know, the busier we get, the easier it is for days and seasons to fly by. It can be tempting to prioritize study sessions or meetings for clubs that boost your resume. But don't let your desire for future success keep you from embracing the unique opportunities you have in college. How often will you be immersed in a community of other thoughtful individuals who are living and learning together?

Of course, we cannot spend all our time in these settings at the expense of our studies and commitments. In fact, it is important to set boundaries to protect your time and wellbeing. Healthy boundaries allow us to show up in conversations as our best selves, offering our listening attention and thoughtful insight because we have the energy to do so.

But more often than not, we can take a few minutes out of our day or an hour out of our week to deepen our relationships with the people we love. And these conversations don't have to be fancy. They can happen in all sorts of places, as we are living our ordinary lives. I recall honest moments with friends as we shared prayers in dorm rooms, stories of heartache on long road trips, reflections on loss in the dining hall, and questions about the mystery of faith under the stars as we swung on hammocks at the park. Sometimes, we will seek out these life-giving conversations and other times, we will find ourselves in them—a moment of recognition falling upon us as we see with pristine clarity that these are the deep places of connection our souls have been longing for.

These intimate spaces not only draw us toward others but also allow time for personal reflection. We can ask ourselves questions like: *How have my experiences shaped the person I am today? What are the values I hold most dear? Who do I want to become? And how can I pursue a meaningful life within a loving community?*

It may be easier to move through our days without examining our motivations and desires. But it is the very process of doing so that adds a profound level of meaning to the ordinary tasks we are performing. So let us step into these opportunities to reflect on the lives we are living and the people we want to grow into. And let us be thankful when we get to do this in a community.

CHAPTER 3

CLDS AND VIDEO ESSAYS

On Engaging in Our Education

Dear resident,

I was sitting in a small room on the top floor of one of BC's oldest buildings. The sky was dark outside the window, contrasting the fluorescent light above me. Pages of assigned reading were sprawled out on the desk in front of me. As I checked the clock, a growing sense of panic fluttered in me. I was exhausted. All I wanted to do was fall into bed and forget my responsibilities. But I needed to do something. So, I skimmed the reading as quickly as I could before packing my backpack and trudging back to my dorm.

I couldn't help but wonder, *How did I get here?*

I remember printing out the syllabus, reading every line, and imagining how fascinating each reading assignment would be. During the first week of classes, I took detailed lecture notes, engaged in enriching conversations with my peers, and immersed myself in assignments with great care. I wasn't afraid to work hard in that class. I cared about the subject and recognized the privilege of learning from a dedicated professor.

But over time, the class became more difficult. My insecurity about my performance rose, triggering feelings of anxiety, stress, and sometimes even dread. As my schedule got busier, I often zoned out during lectures or disengaged from the class discussion to work on other projects that needed my attention.

And suddenly there I was, with just a few weeks left in the semester. My only goal was to get a good grade so that all my hard work would not go to waste. I no longer cared about interacting with the material in a thoughtful way or going above and beyond in the class. And a question I found myself pondering at various times throughout college emerged in my mind: *How did my enthusiasm for this class dwindle so much from when I began?*

With honesty,
Elizabeth

The elephant in the room

As I began considering what I wanted to share with you about engaging in our educational experience, I knew it was important for me to acknowledge the elephant in the room: although we attend college to learn, we do not always enjoy the actual "learning process."

As you read in my letter, even though I loved school, I went through periods where I felt burned out in my classes.

Looking back, I know it is normal for stress to grow as we move through the semester or quarter, affecting our attentiveness. But when this stress gets too high, we can become overwhelmed. And when we do, we develop a mindset of "pushing through" our classes. Instead of showing up to learn, we merely see our classes as a means to achieving an end goal (success).

Manifestations of this approach include:

- Choosing easy classes that will boost our GPA but will not challenge us to think critically

- Doing the bare minimum to complete our assignments and pass our classes

- Letting our attention wander or distracting ourselves during the limited class time when we should be learning

- Keeping our heads down in class because socializing takes up time and energy

- Creating generic work rather than bringing our unique perspective and voice to assignments and discussions

I am not claiming to have avoided these behaviors, nor do I believe that we should aim for perfection and enthusiastic participation in every single class. But I do think that we miss out on the unique offerings of a college education when this mindset becomes our default.

In this chapter, I will share the discoveries I have made about the power of curiosity, connection, and creativity to enrich our academic journeys. I hope that the following stories will inspire you to lean into your educational pursuits with renewed excitement. **As you will quickly realize, many of our classes do not feel particularly "meaningful" on the surface. Instead, it is our purposeful engagement with the material and the people we work alongside that gives our learning experience meaning.**

Find the courage to follow your curiosity

I still remember sitting at the small desk in my Spanish residencia during my junior year abroad as I spoke on a video call with the dean of BC's graduate School of Social Work. After stumbling upon an interesting article on the school's website about system dynamics, I emailed the department to learn more. To my surprise, I received a reply from the dean's office inviting me to chat. Between spotty Wi-Fi interruptions, I listened with intrigue as he explained this fascinating approach to understanding and intervening in complex systems. At the end of the call, he told me about a class the school was offering in the spring called Community-Based System Dynamics. And much to my delight, he said it was open to undergrads.

A few months later, back in the States, I walked up several flights of stairs to our first class in Gasson Hall with a mixture of anxiety and excitement. Taking a seat in one of the chairs that our instructor Kelsey had arranged for us, I looked around at my classmates, feeling intimidated by their maturity. But as the class began, my nerves settled, and I felt more comfortable participating. Unlike many of my other courses, that first class was very engaging, allowing us to dive into key concepts through conversation and experimentation. I even had the chance to draw my first of many causal loop diagrams (CLDs) on a large Post-it pad. And as I emerged from Gasson into the cold January air, I knew I was in for something special.

Over the next few months, I loved learning how to map and analyze complex systems. I appreciated Kelsey's intentional design of the course, which translated theoretical concepts into practical applications. With each class, I felt like I was simultaneously gaining more knowledge and growing my interest in the subject. It was as if I had opened one door and realized with excitement that it led to two more doors just waiting to be opened.

When the course ended, I reached out to Kelsey to see whether she had any research opportunities available—and she said yes! As a result, I worked as her research assistant for the next year, helping her plan and facilitate several virtual sessions. We collaborated with teams who were supporting low-income senior employment, STEM education in prisons, and families experiencing homelessness in Boston. Our discussions and the nuanced discoveries that arose from them captivated me. And I felt privileged to work on those projects with such wise, creative, and devoted individuals.

As I reflect on that amazing journey, which I never expected to go on when I entered college, I know it all started when I sent that email. Put simply, it began when I followed my curiosity.

When I think about curiosity, I remember my younger self. Before grades and comparisons and the invisible checklist of tasks you must complete to obtain your dream job, there was pure, uninhibited curiosity. Not only does it generate excitement for learning inside us, but it reminds us that we have not yet arrived at a place of mastery.

As you enter college, you may be tempted to only sign up for courses in which you know you will succeed. Maybe this temptation arises from a very understandable desire to do well. Or it could come from the inadequacy you feel as you try to measure yourself against your high-achieving classmates. Whatever the case, I invite you to reframe your personal definition of success. What if success was measured by *growth* instead of perfection?

This "growth mindset" places far more value on your overall transformation from beginning to end, rather than demanding a constant "success rate" throughout the course. When we give ourselves permission to be "beginners," we expand our capacity to face unknown situations with humility, open-mindedness, and perseverance. This adaptability is invaluable in a constantly changing world. While you may not see the immediate results of this long-term growth mindset, it will ultimately serve you for the rest of your life.

Now, what does this look like practically? And how do we balance this call to follow our curiosity with our desire to perform well in our classes? For me, this looked like signing up for a few courses that would push me outside my comfort zone and a few in which I believed I could do well. This mindset allowed me to grow in courage and confidence, which are both valuable on our learning journeys.

While some may advocate that you should just "push through" your classes, this is not compatible with curiosity. Instead, curiosity requires outward attentiveness and internal reflection—and these things take intention and time to take root and grow. While it may be easier to move through our academic career with our eyes fixed on one rigid plan, consider how much we will miss out on: the chance to ask questions, discover new learning methods, and uncover interests we did not even realize we had.

Open the gift of connection

Sometimes, it is easier to show up to class, sit at the back, and keep to ourselves. Especially when we are tired or stressed, attempting to engage in convivial conversation feels more burdensome than worthwhile. But engaging with classmates and professors in a personalized way adds a spark of excitement to the otherwise mundane days that are inevitable over the course of our learning journeys. And ultimately, these connections remind us what a gift it is to learn and grow in a community.

Indeed, I can't imagine my educational experience without the classmates I learned alongside. Sometimes, my peers offered a much-needed reprieve from the monotony of a 2.5-hour lecture through humorous comments or ordinary exchanges about our lives. Other times, they reminded me that I was not alone in my confusion. I remember the relief I felt when I turned to someone sitting beside me and asked, "Do you understand this?" Either they laughed and said, "Honestly, not really," or they kindly took the time to explain it to me. In both scenarios, I felt immediately less insecure and alone, remembering that I was not there to prove my perfect mastery over the material but to learn, just like everyone else.

Not only can we connect with our classmates, but our professors can be an enormous source of encouragement. They offer us much-needed perspective from "beyond" these four years and provide wise counsel as we discern how our academic interests might inform our future careers. Despite the advances in learning technology, we are not yet learning from robots. It is a privilege to learn from people who care about us, challenge us, and see our potential—even when we can't see it in ourselves.

It is also pertinent that we remember to see them not just as instructors but as people. I loved noticing the mannerisms and interests that my professors brought to class. One of my professors walked into our morning class every week with a bottle of Diet Coke; another played lively music at the beginning of class; and another hid math memes in his slideshows. I hope you too can keep an eye out for the specific ways that your professors thoughtfully design classes to foster engagement and reveal their individual personalities.

I also remember how my professors showed me kindness. When I completed my senior year from home during the coronavirus pandemic, I worried about the effects of the distance on my ability to fully engage with my classmates and professors. And yet, I recall the ways that my professors went above and beyond to make sure the experience was valuable and enjoyable for students who joined virtually. Professor Field greeted me by name as I entered the Zoom conference and often asked me about my week or the weather in California. This small gesture was her way of saying, "You belong in this class, and we are happy you are here."

Now, I cannot promise you that every professor will be particularly engaging. More than likely, you will have professors you are not fond of. There are many possible reasons for this. Maybe you disagree with their outspoken religious or political beliefs. Perhaps they struggle to teach the material well, grade harshly, or don't foster a collaborative environment. My advice in these instances is to lean into whatever makes the class come alive for you. Maybe it is a study group that you create with your peers to help each other through confusing material and bond over your misery. Or perhaps it is the subject itself that, although poorly taught, still fascinates you. If this is the case, don't hesitate to look for other resources to supplement the professor's lectures, such as teaching assistants, a tutor, or an enriching textbook.

Ultimately, the concept of "pushing through" our classes is not compatible with creating meaningful connections either. To pursue connection, we must look up from our work and really see the people in the room with us. I invite you to look for these opportunities in your classes, however small they may be. Wouldn't it be amazing if the classroom could be a space for transformation, not only in your learning journey but also in your relationships?

Embrace your creative potential

During my last semester of college, I signed up for a nonfiction creative writing course. Although I loved creative writing when I was young, a fair amount of time had passed since I had intentionally done it. Yet, that class reinvigorated a pure love of writing in me. To show up each week and write freely, gather with gifted and warm-hearted individuals, and have an excuse to dive into the recesses of my mind and weave gems of memory into stories—what could be better?

For the final assignment of the semester, our professor Kim gave us the freedom to produce an essay in whatever form we wanted. Some students wrote a traditional essay, others opted for artistic collages that incorporated writing and images, and I made a video essay. For much of the class, I had written about individuals who had inspired or influenced me. But for that final essay, I shared more personal stories.

Over the course of a few weeks, I recorded footage around my town, compiled special memories into a montage, and added a voiceover to weave them together. While this production required much more time and effort than a written essay, I delighted in the process, and I came to see my project more as a labor of love than a homework assignment. The cherry on top was the warm reception I received from my classmates, whose feedback I had grown to value tremendously.

As I reflect on this project, I remember the satisfaction that arose from creating something I was proud of and can enjoy even to this day.

This is how I want to approach the work that matters to me. I want to embrace the remarkable act of creativity to share work that is both authentic and meaningful. I want to "express myself" *and* to affect others.

Like curiosity, creativity is ingrained in many of us at a young age. But as we grow older, it becomes more difficult to find environments that foster creative exploration. Our collective loss of creativity is one of the most unfortunate results of the growing societal pressure to follow a very specific "path to success" in college and beyond.

I understand the temptation to look around at your classmates' projects or study habits and seek to emulate their approaches. Of course, there is a place for this, especially in classes with more rigid structures. But I implore you not to suppress your unique perspective and individual expressions of creativity to appease your parents, impress your classmates, or fit into a mold for the "type of person" you think you should be. Although we live in a culture that often bends toward conformity, we *can* stand firm against the current.

As I discovered in my writing class, when we generate truly original work, we often enjoy the process more *and* create high-value projects. What would it look like for you to see beyond traditional patterns of thinking as you engage in your classes? How might your life experiences, the subjects that pique your curiosity, and your ambitions for the future all contribute to the unique lens through which you see the world? It is from this perspective that your creativity can emerge—and with it, the stories that only you can tell.

Remember the gift you opened

I hope these stories and reflections have given you a fresh perspective on the privilege of learning in a classroom alongside other passionate individuals. May you feel a sense of relief that you don't have to project enthusiasm 24-7 and can instead appreciate even the most "boring" classes and seemingly mundane days. This appreciation does not have to arise from the surface appearance of your classes but from the gifts they hold for you if you are willing to look a little closer.

Even in the classes that you are less excited about, try to show up with a posture of expectation and a readiness to learn. Learning can take many forms. You can learn which subjects you love and which don't interest you; you can learn how to grow your confidence and how to make space for others to grow theirs; you can learn to ask for help and offer help to your classmates; and you can learn to show up when you feel less than your best, remembering that you are worthy of love regardless of your performance.

I remember that feeling of sitting in a 2.5-hour lecture, eyes glazing over as I looked at the clock on the wall, wondering whether I could get it to move any faster. I know what it is like to wish we could skip ahead to the next break or even to the summer when things have slowed, and we can catch our breath. But try to take a moment to catch your breath now and remember the gift you opened in the first place.

I opened that letter from BC on a Sunday evening in my small California city. It was mid-March of my senior year of high school, and my friend Steffi and I were walking through a parking lot toward our cars. Halfway between the street behind us and my old Toyota Camry ahead, I stopped in my tracks as I saw a new email pop up in my inbox.

Sender: Boston College Admissions

Too excited to wait until I was home, I opened the email and read those sweet words: "Dear Elizabeth, I am delighted to offer you admission to the Carroll School of Management at Boston College."

What a joyous day that was!

My wish for you is that you will never forget the gift you opened when you entered college. May you not roll your eyes at the person in the front row who always raises their hand, but let this person challenge you to ask your own questions. May your desire to learn replace your need to be right, and may your appreciation for your teacher's care and commitment lend you grace for them when their lectures feel long and dull (because sometimes they will). May your classmates become friends who open your eyes to see a new world— one that is full of more possibility, beauty, and love than you saw before. May you step into each class like you are crossing a threshold into a sacred space of transformation. May you become like a sponge as you soak in wisdom and search for truth. May you find the courage to ask hard questions and sit with uncertainty. And may you leave each class with gratitude as if it were your last class. Because someday it will be.

CHAPTER 4

CHAMOMILE TEA AND "T" RIDES

On Slowing Down

Dear resident,

On an October morning of my sophomore year, I walked to the bus stop after my weekly service placement at Rosie's Place, a women's homeless shelter in Boston. As I covered the short distance of a few blocks, a wave of exhaustion washed over me. Serving in the overnight shelter meant that I usually only got a few hours of sleep.

If it was any other day of my week, I would have to rush back to campus for class or a meeting. But it was not any other day. That day was a Friday. And it was my Sabbath.

Despite my fatigue, I was excited. The night before, I had made a plan to visit a café in Cambridge and then explore a thrift store nearby. The bus dropped me off just a few stores away from the café. As I opened the door, I immediately felt at ease. I walked over to the counter

47

where I ordered a tall cup of chamomile tea and micro-wavable oatmeal.

The café was fairly empty that early in the morning as I walked over to a couch against the wall and placed my food on a small square table with a potted plant on top. Taking a deep breath, I settled on the couch and opened the memoir I had recently started reading. I was in my happy place. Reading for fun, with no pressing engage-ments to pull me back to campus, I felt my body finally begin to rest at the end of a busy week. What a rare gift it was to be present in my body, not needing to think beyond the present moment.

Sometime within the next hour, I looked up to see an older woman wander in with her small, black dog. She wore a large coat, a long scarf, glasses, and a necklace with aquamarine stones. Her graying hair was pulled up loosely into a bun. I couldn't help but notice that she resembled many of the women I had spent time with at Rosie's Place, and I wondered if she, too, was experiencing homeless-ness. After gazing around the café, she approached the corner where I was sitting and asked whether she could sit in the chair near me.

"Of course!" I said. And then we began to chat.

She introduced herself as Dana, and we spoke for about an hour, sharing stories from our pasts, reflections on the present, and hopes for the future. I learned that she was, in fact, experiencing homelessness. She expressed her love for her sweet dog, who was her loyal companion during many long days and nights. And I remember how a wide smile lit up her entire face as she spoke. It surprised me how comfortable I felt speaking with Dana, despite our many differences. It was like we were old friends, checking in on each other and showing genuine concern for one another's wellbeing.

After a heartfelt goodbye, I grabbed my backpack and headed out the front door. I walked a few blocks to the thrift shop where I perused piles of clothes before returning to campus. Throughout the day, my mind continued to wander to that conversation in a Cambridge café. I was so grateful for the chance to start my day in such a meaningful way. Although I had planned to enjoy a quiet morning reading, meeting Dana was far from an annoying interruption. No—it was more like a surprising encounter with grace. And I can't help but wonder whether I would have made time to sit with her and truly listen to her story if I had been in a hurry.

With peace,
Elizabeth

From hurrying to cherishing restful days

As I look back on my sophomore year (arguably my busiest year of college), I am thankful for the decision I made to carve out Fridays as my day of rest. Make no mistake—for most of my life, I was not the poster child for intentional rest. If anything, I was the epitome of a "busy bee." I had built a fast-paced life for myself and enjoyed the sense of purpose that my never-ending to-do list gave me. Sure, I sometimes felt overwhelmed and walked dangerously close to burn-out. But isn't that just an inevitability in our modern world?

It wasn't until the summer before my sophomore year that I developed an interest in the Christian practice of Sabbath. As I listened to a series of sermons on the topic, the pastor's reflections on the value of soul-nourishing rest enticed me. Instead of Sabbath feeling restrictive as it always had, it appealed to me for several reasons: the gift of resting in God's love, the freedom of a loosely scheduled day, the permission to release my tight grip on control and constant productivity, the opportunity to rediscover the creativity that simmers inside us during times of rest, and the chance to *just be* with the people I love.

And so, I began taking Fridays as a Sabbath. Along with exploring cafés in the city, I enjoyed riding the "T" (Boston's subway system), taking afternoon naps, painting with friends, going to a movie theater, and embarking on peaceful walks around the reservoir. Some days I baked cookies, and on others, I enjoyed a meal out with friends. As I moved through the day, I asked myself questions like, *What does my body need right now? What will be restful? What will allow me to experience delight?* I remember feeling unhurried during those Fridays— and I realize how rare that experience is in our fast-moving culture.

While slowing down looked like practicing Sabbath for me, it may look different for you. I encourage you to take up a practice that is authentic to you and your beliefs. As you do, I hope you will experience the restorative power of rest, especially during this busy season of your life.

Through this practice, although done imperfectly, I came to discover what I was missing before. **While I used to believe that I would** find meaning in my life by rushing ahead toward my ambitions, I realized that slowing down allows us to cherish the gifts available to us in the present moment. These gifts look like connection, natural beauty, and rejuvenating rest, which we often neglect or take for granted despite the value they bring to our lives.

This emphasis on the present brings to mind words from a prayer book I received as a gift from my high school English teacher. A portion of the morning prayer reads, "Help us to embrace possibility, respond graciously to disappointment and hold tenderly those we encounter. Help us be fully present to the day."[1] As I remember those special Fridays of my sophomore year, these words feel like an encapsulation of the sacred moments of connection I had with friends and strangers alike. And yet, so many of us miss out on these sacred experiences because we have bought into a false narrative about success that draws us away from a truly meaningful life.

Recognizing the flaws in our current narrative

Four years may sound like a long time, but believe me, it can pass in the blink of an eye. How strange, then, that when we look around at many of our classmates, they are rushing off to the next class, club meeting, or study session without pausing to enjoy where they are in the present moment. Rather than judge ourselves and our classmates for our hurried pace of life, it is helpful to consider what has contributed to this narrative we are adhering to.

Maybe a part of us understands that our time is limited—and this is why we try so hard to pack in all our responsibilities, social gatherings, and study sessions. We worry we will miss out on an essential part of college if we take a moment to slow down. I know how easy it is to fall into the mindset of "if I just work harder and smarter, I

can somehow maximize my time and fit more goodness into my life."
Maybe you too have experienced this pull toward "more and more"
in response to your fear of missing out.

Of course, many of us hustle so we can accomplish our big ambitions. We absorb this subtle belief from the surrounding culture that
slowing down prevents us from reaching our goals for success and
fulfillment. And this belief leads us to tire ourselves out, trying not
to disappoint ourselves and those we love.

Finally, many of us tie our self-worth to our output level. My
friend Josie reflected on her struggle with this, explaining, "I've struggled with 'being busy' my whole life. But then in college, the struggle
was even worse. I felt validated and affirmed when I was constantly
busy. But I was finding my worth in what I was doing, which is
never a good thing and ultimately causes people to crash and burn."
Her words illuminate why so many of us get to college and find that
we are racing just as hard as—if not harder than—we were in high
school. Because not only do we enter college with this ingrained
mindset, but the culture around us praises us for practicing the very
habits that leave us feeling worn out and unfulfilled.

As you look at each of these motivations for embracing "hurry"
as the norm, is there one that resonates most with you? Are you
driven by a fear of missing out, a fixation on your big ambitions, or
the temptation to identify with your productivity? Or maybe a little of each? The intense emotions surrounding these explanations
make sense because this stage of our lives feels so consequential. But I
learned that there are flaws in the narrative I had been telling myself.
There is actually a better way to live. And I suspect it might even
help us meet the very desires that motivated us to embrace "hurry"
in the first place.

When we are afraid of missing out

When we try to fill our schedules to the brim, we find ourselves juggling our activities instead of enjoying them. As "hurry" drains our energy, our capacity to cherish the experiences that we had enthusiastically said yes to shrinks. It is like sitting in front of a delectable chocolate cake, meant to be savored with each bite that melts in your mouth. Then, you suddenly realize you are in an eating competition, and instead of indulging in the dessert in front of you, you are frantically piling mounds of cake into your mouth, unable to distinguish between the intricate layers of flavor woven into the delicacy. In a podcast with Greg McKeown, the author of *Essentialism*, his guest Kyle Westaway shared these wise words: "The quality of our yeses is dictated by the quantity of our nos."[2] This wisdom turns our culture's obsession with quantity upside down and replaces it with a much worthier endeavor: building a life based on quality experiences that enrich us instead of depleting us.

When we are driven by big ambitions

When we fear that slowing down will prevent us from reaching our admirable goals for success, we forget that maybe rest is exactly what we need to recharge. Upon resting, we rediscover lost wisdom, reacquaint ourselves with joy, and renew our sense of purpose. I hope you hear me when I say this: my intention with these chapters is to invite you into deeper experiences of meaning, hope, and love in a culture that holds up success and achievement as the ultimate prizes. But this doesn't mean I believe that accomplishing our goals is a bad thing. In fact, there are many worthwhile dreams we aspire to reach. So, I will share a secret that I learned when I finally did slow down: slowing down did not inhibit me from succeeding. Rather, I was able to perform better in my classes and accomplish the goals I set for myself when I built a rhythm of rest into my week. With this balanced approach, I prioritized long-term flourishing over short-term bursts of adrenaline and accomplishment.

When we identify with our productivity

When we tie our self-worth to our productivity and "value output," we miss out on the opportunity to *just live.* In her book *How to Do Nothing,* Jenny Odell says, "Solitude, observation, and simple conviviality should not be recognized only as ends in and of themselves, but inalienable rights belonging to anyone lucky enough to be alive."[3] It is unfortunate that this mindset toward enjoying life seems taboo in modern society. While we may not be able to change an entire culture, we can change the way we as individuals behave. And this matters. I have to believe this matters. You see, intentional rest carves out a new path in the middle of the well-worn road. By making it a priority, we are breaking the hold that the productivity-obsessed culture has on us. When we get off a treadmill, it has no choice but to stop moving. Similarly, it is our choice to slow down our pace of life, and when we do, the race loses its power over us. Odell's words remind me that we are here to live, not just to produce. We are here to love and be loved, to see beauty, and to delight in the goodness that is right at our fingertips. We are not defined by what we create or contribute. Rather, these things can be just one part of what it means for us to live out our purpose, not the whole.

Finding a way to breathe again

One of the most valuable lessons I learned in college is that just because the culture around me praises hurry and hustle does not mean I need to. College feels like a consequential time because in a way, it is the final step in our preparation for our adult lives. I think the secret that so many of us don't realize until it is too late is that in college, we do not just learn how to write stories or crunch numbers or market a product. We also learn what is important to us and practice devoting our time and attention to these things.

It might be tempting to look at your peers and assume they are successfully juggling exciting social lives, a rigorous course load, and a plethora of extracurricular activities. You might look at their busy agendas—color-coded and planned to a T—and conclude that a busy life is a full life. But if you try to keep up with all the "shoulds" (go out every weekend, ace all your tests, go to the gym five times a week, etc.), you may come to find that you are not actually enjoying any of it.

I am beginning to believe that a full life is one where we can breathe fully. Because there is room for this. It is a life where we have space to cultivate wonder, be curious, explore new cafés, and sit down with strangers because we are not cramming for an exam or rushing off to the next appointment on our agenda.

In a world where we love to work and create, plan and produce, I felt most alive on those Fridays when I could see and taste and listen. When I could slow down long enough to blend into the slower rhythms of nature around me, to find myself lost in the greater story of this city, and to realize that sometimes we must loosen our grip on control to find peace. It may seem paradoxical, but I have been able to find deep fulfillment in my life by intentionally emptying my schedule at regular intervals to rest and reset.

What do you need to remove from your life so you can make space for rest and rejuvenation? What are the elements of your life that are filling you with restlessness instead of peace? I am not saying you should quit any of your classes or important commitments. Perhaps this change does not need to be drastic. You could start by carving pockets of rest into your schedule, even if they are incredibly small at first. Whatever this process looks like for you, don't wait until life slows down on its own. Because the odds are high that if you wait for the perfect time to start, the time will never come.

For me, this intentional change involved disentangling my identity and worth from my productivity output. I also had to overcome the temptation to fill my schedule on Fridays—even with good things—because I knew how beneficial this practice would be for the rest of the week. Of course, many of the activities I devoted my time to were worthwhile and meaningful, but if we focus too much on pursuing every individual good thing, we miss out on the experience of having a good life as a whole. I want to be a whole person—and I think this begins with discerning where my limits are.

Living moment by moment

Take some time to reflect on how the culture around you is influencing the way you spend your time. As you do this, maybe you can release some of the written or unwritten "rules" you have been adhering to. May you feel a newfound sense of possibility and freedom as you ask yourself what you can let go of to embrace the gift of rest in your week—and all it may create space for. Once you have slowed to a quiet pace, you can begin to look around and ask yourself, *What is available to me in the present that will be life-giving?*

These answers will be different for each of us, and I think that is beautiful. When we step away from the never-ending work cycle of our culture, we do not just release its hold over us, but we also step into our own unique identity. We finally have space to consider what activities we do enjoy, how much rest we need based on our particular physical and emotional needs, and who will fill up our energy tank instead of draining it.

As I think back to that unique season of my life, I realize that not only did I enjoy the activities I took part in on my Sabbath, but I also liked the person I was becoming. It was as if I was rekindling a friendship with my former self—the one who didn't yet know what it cost to live according to the world's standards for success instead of her own. Perhaps what was buried underneath performance and comparison and frantically scribbled to-do lists finally had space to breathe. To emerge from its hiding place and reveal a forgotten depth within me to myself and those I love. I liked this version of myself— the one who was more thoughtful, open to the people around me, and observant of the small, beautiful interactions in my path that I often missed when I was moving too fast.

Annie Dillard said, "How we spend our days is, of course, how we spend our lives. What we do with this hour, and that one, is what we are doing."[4] As I found myself slowing down enough to be present for my life as it was, I finally came to understand these words in a fresh way. For so long, I had viewed my life in seasons: *I am spending these years as a high school student, I am spending my summer at camp, I am spending the spring as a lacrosse player, I am spending four years as a college student.* But there was something that felt off about those declarations, as if they were overgeneralizations of who I was, missing the nuance and specificity in the life I was really living.

And so, once a week, during one of the busiest periods of my college journey, I slowed down long enough to begin framing the activities of my life in a new way: *I am walking to the bus stop after spending a night hearing stories from women whom I will never be able to forget. I am drinking hot tea among strangers and yet I feel perfectly at home. I am walking around the reservoir as the bright white clouds and blue sky reflect off the water. I am small compared to this great big, beautiful city that flies by my window on the "T," and I wouldn't have it any other way. I am at a winter concert supporting dear friends as they sing beautiful music. I am quiet and I love this version of me—the one who doesn't always need to speak and recognizes beauty in a chorus of voices. I am this person who lives hour by hour, moment by moment on this day, for this day is all I am promised. And it is a good day.*

CHAPTER 5

EMMA'S SURPRISE

On the Joy of Generosity

Dear resident,

When I was a sophomore, I was involved in a college ministry group through a local church. Toward the end of the year, my friend Emma began fundraising for a service trip she was taking to India that summer. One morning in early May, I woke up to a GroupMe notification that I had been added to a group chat. The first message explained that Emma had 12 more days to raise her full amount, and we were going to try to raise half of it by the end of the day, unbeknownst to her!

I smiled, thankful for the sweet community I had found myself in—one that was filled with a passionate and generous spirit, believing we could all come together to bless our friend as she embarked on this adventure. As the day continued, group members added their friends to the chat until it had over 100 people in it. I was amazed by the enthusiasm that began with one message and continued to spread as more and more people joined. At around 4:30 p.m., I received a message that not only had we raised our goal for the end of that day, but we had fully funded the rest of Emma's trip. Now, we were ready to surprise her with the news!

About 20 of us gathered in Emma's suite that evening for the surprise. We set up food, hung a celebratory poster, blew up balloons that floated around the room, and chatted excitedly as we prepared for her arrival.

When we knew Emma was nearby, we shut off the lights and tried our best to remain silent. I was standing on top of her wooden table beside a few other people, filming the surprise. From the suppressed giggles and the energy that was mounting in the darkness, we knew we were a part of something special. We heard her footsteps before a sliver of light emerged as she opened the door. In a flash, we turned the room lights on and greeted her in song.

Her face lit up with a mixture of surprise, excitement, and bewilderment. We handed her a package of naan bread because it is a staple in India. She sifted through it until she found one with the final amount that we had raised written in Sharpie. As Emma stood in her kitchen in disbelief, we expressed our gratitude for her and blessed her trip. Her expression shifted back and forth between joy and that look you get right before you cry. After cheering for her, we stayed in her suite a while longer, enjoying one another's company and the treats we had brought to celebrate this special occasion.

With joy,
Elizabeth

The temptation of self-focus

This experience impressed upon me the gift of belonging to a community that lives generously and celebrates the people who are a part of it. While this realization may seem obvious, it took me a while to learn what I had to let go of to fully accept this gift.

Growing up, I was influenced by a culture that encouraged individual success and visible displays of accomplishment to "prove" our worth. While we often think of greed in a financial context, another form can be just as toxic: devoting most of our time, energy, and attention to our self-improvement and ambitions. The danger of this self-focused mindset is that we are less attentive to the needs of others. When our main ambition is to prop ourselves up, straining toward a goal of perfection that will never be attainable, we miss out on the opportunity to uplift others. If I could return to my high school years, I would spend a little less time chasing success and a little more time encouraging the people around me.

I now believe that an essential part of living a meaningful life is embracing the opportunities we have to be generous with both our time and our resources. Generosity draws us outward toward others in love, offering us meaningful connection and freedom as we release our fixation on our own needs and desires.

Each one of us has a different financial situation and a unique relationship with generosity. But as I share my journey, I hope you will reflect on the role that generosity might play in your time at college and beyond.

Waking up to a world beyond myself

Maybe it would be simpler if there was one transformative moment when I went from living a self-focused life to deeply caring about the wellbeing of others. But in reality, waking up to a world beyond myself took many years. It looked more like falling asleep and waking up again and then sleepwalking and then waking up yet again.

I suppose it began when I was young. I can still remember standing behind a table with my parents and my older brother as we served Costco lasagna in tin foil pans and Caesar salad with crunchy croutons to strangers. My parents took us to a homeless shelter to serve dinner occasionally. I don't remember everything about those evenings, but I remember that I enjoyed them. And though I did not understand the complexities of homelessness, I knew that showing up to serve food to strangers mattered.

As I grew older and entered high school, I continued to enjoy service. Whether I was tutoring younger students or serving at a local homeless shelter, the work I did felt purposeful. And yet, I was blind to the many ways I made that work about myself. At a time when volunteering and resume-building often went hand in hand, it was hard to disentangle my self-interests from the needs of the people I encountered.

When I was in college, I shed some of my preconceived notions of service. As my motivations shifted, I focused less on the appearance of volunteer work and more on the essence of it. I suppose I can attribute this shift to several things: learning from people I looked up to who served with humility, developing a maturity that comes with age, and recognizing my own biases. But if I am being honest, my heart posture metamorphosed most when I came face-to-face with the devastation of poverty. In those moments, I no longer saw people I could serve to boost my ego. I just saw fellow humans who were hurting. And I will share one such story with you.

During the summer after my freshman year of college, I took an international trip to visit some organizations my church partnered with. One day, we were driving through a large, busy capital city. When traffic came to a pause, a group of young men approached our van, tapping against the side windows and holding out their hands for money. After a little while, they retreated through the street and sat down on the curb. As we drove away, one of our local companions told us these men sit on the side of the road, sniffing glue to stave off the ache of hunger that has become their everyday reality. There was something about that exchange that shocked me. I knew that many people in my community back home and in the country I was visiting experienced food insecurity and hunger. But coming face-to-face with young people who knowingly inhaled harmful substances to cope with hunger pains felt different.

Maybe you have also encountered poverty or pain that forever changed you. Maybe you have begun to wonder what to do with the heavy emotions these experiences birthed inside you. Perhaps they are even overwhelming. This does not make you weak. Opening ourselves up to the transformative power of compassion is not pain-free, but it is significant. And I believe it is worth it.

It can be scary to admit what we know now. It can be uncomfortable to continue moving within the spheres of our lives when we realize ours is not the only reality that exists. What do we do when we catch a glimpse of suffering without the buffer of a television screen? What do we do when we come face-to-face with the truth?

What is my responsibility?

One of BC's most popular classes is called Person and Social Responsibility (or "PULSE" for short). Predominantly taken by sophomores, this course combines immersive service-learning placements with classroom teachings on philosophy and theology. Throughout the year, we were encouraged to examine our beliefs about significant topics like justice, service, community, and compassion. One of the questions we explored was, *What is my personal responsibility to my fellow citizens, both in my local community and in the greater world?*

Among the many things I appreciated about the class's design was the opportunity to discuss our service experiences in small groups each week. I watched my classmates struggle to make sense of the realities they witnessed. Whether we were serving children living in foster care, elderly individuals facing loneliness, or women seeking shelter and social services, each of us encountered stories that were difficult to hear. As we gathered each week, we asked hard questions. We sat in silence when there were no easy answers. We shared stories of heartache and held each other's sorrow with gentle hands. And we wondered how we could give more of ourselves to improve the lives of the people we encountered in our placements.

I don't think the point of that class was to find the perfect answer to the question, *What is my responsibility?* I think it was to find the courage to begin asking it in the first place. Because when we open ourselves to the possible answers to this daring question, we will never be the same. We will no longer be able to walk by a person in need without wondering what we can do to alleviate some of their suffering.

Lately, I have found myself widening the scope of my concern as I consider how I want to use my time and resources. I am learning that there is a difference between caring about others in their suffering and living intentionally so we have the capacity to move from compassion to action. Perhaps living intentionally means allocating some of our resources to causes that will bring long-lasting change in people's lives. Or maybe it means creating a personal "benevolent fund" so we can meet others' needs with joy.

How can you get practical with this concept on your college campus? If you are planning to buy new shoes, maybe you could opt for a less expensive pair. With the remaining money, how about buying a gift for your roommate who is going through a hard time? Or, in addition to tailgating on a Saturday morning, might you also join a friend who is volunteering at a soup kitchen that evening? It doesn't have to be complicated. We don't have to search for the "perfect opportunity" to begin living generously. But when we open our eyes to the opportunities for generosity all around us, we will be surprised by just how meaningful our days can be.

While we often associate responsibility with a heavier burden, when it comes to generosity, I think the result is quite different. What if a deeper compassion for our fellow humans could instill in us a renewed sense of purpose? What if we could wake up each day not only trying to move forward but also ready to offer a hand to someone who feels stuck? What if we could seek out people who are hurting because we see our shared humanity when we look at them? And what if we could invite them to walk forward with us, so we can experience greater freedom together?

The freedom of generous living

When I became an RA, I started to experience the freedom that arises from shifting our focus from our own needs to the needs of others. While I did have to set boundaries, I enjoyed sharing my time and physical space with others. I loved hosting residents in my room for tea and treats, sitting with them as they expressed their fears about the future or wrestled with their friendship conflicts. The more I focused on supporting my residents, the less I cared about the other things that used to occupy my mind, such as my appearance, my desire for external approval, and my fears about the future. By investing in others, I was also investing in my freedom from these preoccupations.

I also looked around me at the individuals who freely gave their resources and time to friends and strangers. Rather than exercising control over their possessions and schedules, they found purpose in sharing them with others. I witnessed a spirit of joy in them as they released their desire for more stuff and greater status. As Maya Angelou said, "I have found that among its other benefits, giving liberates the soul of the giver."[1]

What is it about generosity that breeds freedom? Well, purposeful generosity helps us to relinquish our constant desire for "more." While it might not appear dangerous at first, this obsession with bigger and better can motivate us to prioritize our ambitions over meaningful relationships. But when we choose to live generously, we stop running after an elusive notion of happiness and get to experience the joy of contributing to another person's wellbeing right where we are.

As I remember that spontaneous surprise we orchestrated for Emma, I know I got a glimpse into the freedom that arises when we take our eyes off our own lives for a little while and embrace the chance to celebrate someone else. When I look back at photos and watch videos from that Wednesday night in early May, I can still feel it in my bones: a sense of hope that rose above all my fears. For a short while, my stress about finals and anxieties about the future were suspended, like the balloons hanging beside me as I stood on

the table filming Emma's reaction. And though the stress and anxieties did return later, I got a glimpse into this sweeter way of life.
It was the kind of life in which love and celebration wash away our
fears and worries about the future, reminding us just how small and
fleeting they are in comparison.

The power of communal generosity

It is not easy to make this shift from seeking contentment in plea-
sure, success, and "fitting in" to living generously—nor is it a one-
time choice. Day after day, we get to choose how we want to enter
the world. I love these words from the Catholic Prayer for Generosity:
"Lord, teach me to be generous ... to give and not to count the cost."[2]

What a bold prayer. These words remind us that we need to give
up our desire to "feel generous" to truly reap the benefits of this way of
living. But while I aspire to live this way, I know I fall far short of my
aspirations. I have often counted the cost of my generosity, making note
of my sacrifices as if they made me more worthy of love and respect.

While we may not be able to change our very human desire to
receive recognition for our good deeds, I do think there is power in
participating in communal generosity. Stepping into communal generosity can shift our focus away from how our individual generosity
appears to others or makes us feel. Just as an athlete learns to value
the success of their team over their individual contributions, so too
can we learn how to find our place in a bigger collective.

There are many meaningful opportunities for communal generosity within the college environment. Here are just a few ideas:

- Pitch in with a few friends to pay for a family's meal at a
  restaurant.

- Buy a holiday gift with your fellow residents for an individual who cleans your dorm as an expression of gratitude.

- Purchase a gift with your classmates for your professor at the end of the semester.

- Contribute to an online fundraiser for a classmate who is battling a disease.

When we begin to see our belongings as blessings to be shared instead of hoarded, we experience the gift of living our lives alongside others instead of only for ourselves. This posture also enables us to receive generosity with open hands as we recognize the privilege of being the recipient of love. As we continue to practice generosity in a community, we grow more concerned about the people we connect with than the feeling of significance that our generosity produces.

If you are still struggling with the pride that can accompany giving, I invite you to practice giving anonymously. This could look like leaving flowers outside your friend's door or anonymously donating to a cause online. The less we seek praise for our generosity, the more we can welcome the pure joy of witnessing someone's life being made a little brighter.

The life we make

Norman MacEwen said, "We make a living by what we get, but we make a life by what we give."[3] We are never too young to begin asking ourselves how we want to make a life. What is the legacy we want to leave behind? Do we want to be known as people who pursued success, building a name for ourselves at all costs—or do we want to live an abundant life, choosing to value the good of others above our own achievements?

In college, you will see many people seeking to answer the question, *What is the life I want to make?* Many of us chase the appeal of more until it leaves us burned out and running low on hope. But is it possible to make a life—even more, a remarkable life—by focusing more on what we give than on what we get? I have to believe that it is. I have to believe that what we do with the resources we are blessed with matters.

Are you feeling weighed down by the pressure to figure out your future? If your parents, teachers, or friends keep asking you, "What do you want to do with your life?," begin here. Ask yourself what it would look like to give something away that matters today. Even if it is something small. And pay attention to the joy that arises from this exchange. Joy that stems from generosity does not depend on external markers of success. It cannot be manufactured or replicated in other settings. Rather, it is a particular joy that we walk into by releasing our need to be the center of our own lives.

I know how countercultural this mindset may seem in the college environment where we often design our days around our personal needs and desires. But I have learned that college does not need to be a "cookie-cutter" experience in which you follow a generic path to a diploma without taking risks. You can step outside your comfort zone and discover creative ways to express your love through action. Maybe you will do this on your own—or maybe you will find a community that also values enthusiastic expressions of love.

As you continue on this college journey, I hope you will look for opportunities to step into the miracle of generosity right where you are. Before we have enough resources to give from a place of comfort or become jaded by the opportunities for philanthropy that make us feel significant, we can begin in small ways. May we learn to share our resources joyfully with our roommates, give our time to a classmate who asks for our help in a study session, and share our meals with people who look hungry not only for food but for companionship. And may we understand that generosity is not about us. It is about the person we are loving, one dollar or one slice of naan bread at a time.

CHAPTER 6

MADDY'S DRESSES

On Seeking Justice

*Do your little bit of good where you are; it's those little
bits of good put together that overwhelm the world.*

DESMOND TUTU[1]

Dear resident,

I was at a winter concert in my college chapel on the last
day of November when my friend Maddy leaned over
to me during intermission and said, "I'm so excited for
Dressember this year!"

I looked at her in confusion. "What's Dressember?"

She told me about the Dressember Foundation, an organization that empowers advocates to fight human trafficking through the simple act of wearing a dress every
day of December. This style-based challenge is a fun way
to engage people from across the world in an important
cause. The participants often turn to social media to share
facts about human trafficking along with photos in their

dress. Many participants also find that the simple question, "Why are you wearing a dress in December?" can spark important conversations about the often-misunderstood injustice of modern-day slavery.

Seeing as the next day was December 1, I decided there was no better way to engage in Dressember's work than to jump into the campaign! I gathered the dresses I had, posted about my participation on social media, and asked some friends if I could borrow their dresses.

Over the next 31 days, I walked around in the Boston winter clothed in various dresses. Among those was the pink winter dress I had picked out at a Michigan boutique, an orange-and-black-striped dress from my friend Natasha, a lovely knitted dress from Isabelle, and my favorite pink-and-white dress with a white infinity scarf.

If you are wondering how I wore a dress in a city where the average temperature often dropped below 30 °F, don't worry. I also donned tights, puffy winter coats, gloves, and warm boots. I had no desire to lose feeling in my appendages in my second New England winter.

Despite the cold, I found great delight in participating in Dressember. In a time devoted to studying for finals and wrapping up projects, I enjoyed feeling like each day held a purpose beyond my academic success. I wore a dress when I was studying for finals in the library and shopping for holiday treats at the grocery store. I wore a dress on the airplane to Michigan where I spent Christmas with my family. And yes, I even wore a dress as I played ice hockey on my cousin's lake. I enjoyed seeing Maddy and our friend Wendy wearing their dresses too, reminding me I was not alone in this venture but one of many individuals in this beautiful collective.

During that time, I asked friends and family to financially contribute to the campaign. I was certainly not an expert on the topic, but I enjoyed sharing what I knew on social media and in conversations. I think there is something special about finding a cause we care about and diving into it even when we feel underqualified or overwhelmed by its scope.

When January 1 came around, I slipped back into leggings and a sweater. My 31 days of dresses had come to an end. But my interest in the anti-human trafficking movement had just begun.

Warm regards,
Elizabeth

Justice-seeking is a journey

My participation in Dressember challenged my previous interpretation of what it meant to fight for justice in a world full of injustice. For many years leading up to college, I thought of justice-seeking as a way to make my life matter. I believed that if I could lead a nonprofit or found a social enterprise, then I would fulfill two of my desires: to help heal the hurts that I saw around me and to live a life of significance. My mind was so fixated on a future version of myself that I struggled to see how I could live a mission-driven life right where I was.

At the beginning of my sophomore year, I walked by BC's PULSE office and saw Desmond Tutu's words written on the glass wall: "Do your little bit of good where you are; it's those little bits of good put together that overwhelm the world."

I loved this message so much that I wrote it on the chalkboard hanging on my dorm room door as a reminder that small acts are far more significant than we realize. As I think about my experience with Dressember—and the truth behind those words—I realize that my understanding of purposeful justice work was skewed. Instead, this is what I have come to believe over the past few years: **We do not find satisfaction when we have finally reached our lofty ambitions for "world change and impact" but in the small, everyday steps that we take on this journey toward justice.**

Starting small

Tutu begins with an exhortation to "do your *little bit* of good." At first, this small-step approach was so hard for me to want to follow. I wonder if you feel the same way. I know what it is like to see so much injustice and want—even need—to alleviate the substantial burden it places on the people you care about. But I don't think that Tutu wants us to give up dreaming. Rather, he understands that we must start in small, practical ways. After all, as individuals, we can only do one thing at a time. By asking ourselves what small steps we can take to act upon our convictions, we ensure that we actually begin this work. The alternative, of course, is staying on the observation deck, where the large scope of injustices keeps our feet glued to the ground, unable to do anything.

Along with my participation in Dressember, I took small steps to learn more about the harsh reality of human trafficking. On a summer trip overseas, I met incredible individuals who provided services to survivors of exploitation. At BC, I joined a club dedicated to raising awareness of human trafficking and bringing meaningful discussion around this topic onto our college campus. And during the pandemic, I took part in an online discussion group to learn from members of my community who were fighting human trafficking on a local, national, and international level.

This "little bit" approach encourages us to embrace our smallness with humility. In a culture that praises self-sufficiency, it is tempting to seek recognition for our individual successes, even when we are contributing to a good cause. I have so much grace for my younger self, who deeply desired to do good work and believed that the value of her life was directly tied to what she offered the world. But I had mistaken purposeful work for identity-defining work. I had envisioned justice work as something you rise to, instead of something you humbly step into as a servant. And I am starting to realize that heroism is not the bedrock upon which I want to build my commitment to justice. Deep down, I know that love is a much better motivation than self-righteousness.

When I participated in Dressember, I was humbled by the realization of how small I really am. The simple act of putting on a dress felt insignificant at first—and yet, maybe I needed to learn that it wasn't about me. Rather, I was joining a chorus of advocates around the world, driven by the belief that this combination of joy, creativity, education, and fundraising could actually illuminate the dark places in our world. Acknowledging my smallness was not frightening, although you might imagine it would be. Instead, it was incredibly freeing. When we realize we do not have to carry the burden of injustice alone, we are free to step into the work we are best equipped for—with excitement.

As I think about Tutu's words, I want to emphasize that he says, "Do *your* little bit of good." In doing so, he invites us to discover our specific gifts and interests. Blythe Hill, the founder of Dressember, had a deep desire to combat the injustice of human trafficking. But instead of turning to more traditional avenues like law or social work, she employed her creative vision and love of fashion to begin this amazing initiative.[2] Hill's story reminds us just how powerful both care and passion are in this work. When we are enthusiastic not just about *which* causes we support but also *how* we support them, I believe we can have the greatest impact. As you consider what "*your* little bit of good" may be, I invite you to reflect on these questions:

- Which topics in your classes have you found yourself most intrigued by?

- What interests do you have outside the classroom that you could combine with your passion for a cause?

- Do you have a love of creativity or sports that could fuel your engagement with a particular organization?

- Are there certain subjects that pique your curiosity when you overhear them?

- Is there a specific injustice that you think about often and wonder, *What can I do to help? There must be something I can do!*

Embracing our present opportunities

Perhaps a less emphasized part of Tutu's statement—but just as important—is his encouragement to "do your little bit of good *where you are*." While this may seem obvious, I can't tell you how often I focused on the future work I wanted to do instead of asking myself what was available to me right where I was. Now, I am learning that we do not have to wait until we are fully educated or qualified to engage in the causes we care about. Instead, we can view college as a chance to prepare for our future work *and* step into meaningful opportunities in the present.

It can be easy to look at "world-changers" and believe that we need the perfect credentials and years of experience to make a difference. But I have seen individuals I admire contribute to purposeful causes with a sense of urgency. A writer named Hannah Brencher started the beautiful organization The World Needs More Love Letters after dropping letters in strangers' mailboxes in New York City during a time of loneliness when she was a young adult. Since its founding, this organization has coordinated the delivery of thousands of letters to individuals in need of encouragement from strangers across the world.[3] Likewise, my friend Kyle dedicated himself to climate activism through his participation in a campus club and engagement in local politics. And my classmate Lurein founded a nonprofit called GiveCard during his sophomore year to financially support individuals experiencing homelessness, working with other BC students to make his vision a reality.[4]

The people I admire most are not the ones who just talk about their dreams for the future, always waiting for the perfect opportunity to put their knowledge and experience to good use. Rather, I look up to those who identify a problem they care about and ask themselves what small action they can take in the present moment to begin addressing it. This in no way means they neglect the importance of planning and casting a vision for future work. What it does mean is they do not wait for the perfect set of circumstances to arise before they start engaging in the causes they care about.

I don't want to miss out on my present opportunities for justice work because I am so focused on reaching a "final destination" where I will be satisfied with the impact I have made. I want to live in the tangible reality of the present—even amid disappointments—instead of a mirage of the future. It is in these moments that we interact with individuals who have been affected by injustices. It is in these moments that we come to understand compassion, which means "to suffer with," as being somehow both a sacrifice and a privilege. And it is in these moments—when we look someone in the eyes as we serve them or connect with them—that we realize we are not just talking about "problems" but about people's lives, lives that are worthy of dignity.

Finding purpose in a community

Tutu follows with these words: "*put together*." In recent years, I have come to see the value of being a part of a community of people doing good work, rather than believing that my compassion and empathy necessitate a "heroic" solitary venture. When I surveyed some friends in preparation for a separate writing project, my friend John responded, "I think we should be helping each other live better lives in community, rather than becoming isolated superheroes." John's words reminded me that while my intent to live a life in pursuit of justice and service to others is worthwhile, I miss out on a more meaningful experience if I believe this is a one-person race.

In college, you will be around many people who are doing "world-changing work." Sometimes, this might intimidate you. This was certainly the case when I joined a service-leadership program full of ambitious students and found myself surrounded by future doctors, politicians, and business leaders who were bright, eloquent, hardworking, and driven. But as our friendships developed, I came to see that their genuine desire to care for others motivated them to work hard. As we worked on service projects together later in the program, my feelings of jealousy and inadequacy were replaced by a sense of possibility and excitement. You see, I realized what a privilege it was to be a part of that group of individuals who were committed to using their own gifts for the good of others. My eyes were opened to what jealousy had tried to blind me from: we were stronger together.

When you are tempted to compare yourself with others, becoming envious of those who seem to be "making a bigger impact" than you, pause for a moment. Ask yourself what could be possible if you transformed your jealousy into appreciation and awe. Remember what a gift it is to be surrounded by people who believe that justice is worth fighting for, even though it would be easier to settle for *what is*. Instead of wishing you could have a greater position of influence, try asking yourself, "What are others doing that I can join in? And how can I learn from them?" When you become a participant rather than the star of the show, you can step up to do the work that is right in front of you. And you might be surprised to discover how satisfying the work itself is, however important or unimportant it may appear at first.

When love abounds

This brings us to the end of Tutu's declaration: "that *overwhelm* the world." When I think of the word "overwhelm," I often attach a negative connotation to it. But isn't it beautiful to be a part of something that overwhelms the world with its beauty?

Since Hill founded Dressember in 2013, it has raised over 18 million dollars, providing funding for organizations that support four main pillars: advocacy, prevention, intervention, and survivor empowerment. Since then, over 280,000 people have been involved in the movement as advocates or donors.[5] I love that this movement is fueled by thousands of passionate individuals instead of a few wealthy donors.

Beloved television personality Fred Rogers said, "What changes the world? The only thing that ever really changes the world is when somebody gets the idea that love can abound and can be shared."[6] I wrote these words on a blue sticky note that I placed on the back of my bedroom door. I have read them over and over again and continue to pull inspiration from them. But sometimes I wonder to myself, *Could it really be this simple? Is this belief in the multiplicity of love really strong enough to pour light over the darkest places in our world? And can we trust this light to find tiny holes to break through the seemingly impenetrable walls of injustice?* This is a hard question to wrestle with. Often, the light seems so small compared to the darkness. But I remind myself that simple does not always mean easy. In fact, oftentimes, the simplest convictions we hold as humans are the most difficult to live out. And yet, the difficulty of the road before us does not exempt us from moving forward.

I suppose many people can change the world, and they can find a variety of motivations and a multitude of methods for doing so. But to change the world for good, I think Mr. Rogers is right. I think we need to remember the power of love—to keep it as our deepest motivation and strongest anchor; to embrace it not only as an ideal to aim for but also as a reason to care in the first place. And then, we can rekindle joy as we watch this love proliferate and spread beyond our own reach as it is passed from person to person. In the words of social entrepreneur Becca Stevens, "Love is the most powerful force for change in the world."[7]

Hope as fuel

If justice work begins with love, then I like to think it carries on because of hope. I know it is easy to look at the big problems in the world and feel helpless to make any significant change. But when I find myself feeling weary about this small-step approach to justice, I think of Bryan Stevenson's words: "Hopelessness is the enemy of justice."[8]

Stevenson, a human rights advocate and lawyer, reminds us that we must hold on to hope in this fight. That is why it is so important to remember we are not in this alone. Because if we naively believe that we can change the world on our own, we will be more prone to burnout and despair. Instead, the hope we need to continue this work is available to us when we acknowledge the powerful collective that we are a part of. I know I have found the greatest hope when I see just how much good we can do together.

As you continue this journey, ask yourself what gives you hope. Is it the dedicated collective you find yourself a part of? Is it the small signs of change that you see in your community as a result of the work you put in each day? Is it the feeling you get when you wake up in the morning and know you are living for something greater than yourself? Whatever it is, how can you bring it to mind when you are running low on hope?

When I think of finding hope in the face of injustice, my mind returns to Dressember. As I slipped on a dress each morning, hope bubbled up in me. Sure, I wasn't saving the world. But who among us is called to do that, anyway?

My wish is that you too will experience the hope that arises as we step into the darkest places in our world with courage—not because we are feeling particularly brave, but because countless people have gone before us to lead the way. Look around your campus for opportunities to show up with compassion and enthusiasm. Don't ask yourself what the future version of you will do, or try to mimic the people around you, or believe that you must gain recognition for the work you do to matter. Instead, look for something you can do with joy right where you are. Maybe you want to join a club or a class engaged in grassroots work in your community. Maybe you want to start an organization with a group of friends who have a shared passion for justice. Or maybe you will begin by wearing a dress, not because it feels heroic but because it is an act of hope.

CHAPTER 7

THE ART OF ASSEMBLING PUZZLES

On Searching for a Career

Dear resident,

During the height of the pandemic, my family, like many families, very briefly forayed into the exciting world of "puzzling." One night, my brother, my mom, and I found ourselves huddled over a small game table in the corner of our living room as my dad slept blissfully in his room. We were trying to conquer the puzzle that our neighbor had graciously lent us with pieces designed to construct a satellite image of our neighborhood. The problem was that most of the pieces looked identical—they were either blurry, tan-colored pieces representing the hills in our backyard or dark gray pieces that composed the houses and the street. And what made it even more difficult was that we had challenged ourselves to complete the puzzle without the help of the picture on the box.

As we were all beginning to question our decision to stay up unreasonably late to continue working on the puzzle—an activity that was becoming less and less enjoyable by the second—my brother suddenly exclaimed, "We are not puzzle people!"

We all burst out laughing. This felt like the truest thing anyone had said all night. But despite this acceptance of our lack of puzzling skills, we kept moving forward. While we were not "puzzle people," neither were we people who abandoned our pursuits before we had finished them. So, we forged on, looking meticulously for little clues that would help us move forward. We sorted by color. We tried pulling out the corner pieces and then the edges to create an outline we could work within. We each had different tactics, and we employed them alongside one another, adapting them when needed. Although we couldn't see the final product, we were surprised to find that little by little, the puzzle was beginning to look more like a cohesive picture than randomly scattered pieces.

As I think about my journey of searching for a career, including the classes, internships, and activities I pursued, I realize that the steps I took were a little like putting together a puzzle with no clear picture of the ending. It wasn't until nearly the end of college that I was able to look back on the choices I had made and see how many of them fit together.

Sincerely,
Elizabeth

The appeal of a "perfect plan"

For many years, I didn't understand the importance of leaning into the slow, sometimes arduous work of uncovering our career interests. Instead, I believed that success looked like creating a "perfect plan" and following every step without diverging from it. Maybe you have felt this way too. In our planning-obsessed culture, many of us feel pressured to choose the "perfect path" to our dream job right when we enter college.

I remember sitting in the Eagle's Nest dining hall during my freshman year for an advisor meeting. Staring at the Excel spreadsheet on my laptop, I was determined to plot out each class I would take over the next three and a half years, including the exact semesters when I would take them. *If I can just follow that plan, then my college journey will be a success.* Frankly, I wanted to know what the end of my journey looked like before I got the chance to live it.

But that kind of tight-gripped approach can have unintended consequences. When we are putting together a puzzle, it can be unhelpful to devote excess energy to preparing our strategy before we even open the box. Sometimes, we just have to start laying the pieces down and trust that we will gain further clarity as time passes. **Rather than thinking of choosing a career as taking a one-time photograph, I invite you to liken it to slowly putting together a puzzle through a thoughtful "discovery process."**

The gift of an empty table

When we begin any long journey, we can get so focused on trying to predict every twist and turn ahead that we often forget the gift of an open road—or, in the case of puzzles, an empty table. As I have expressed, I have very little experience putting together puzzles.

But I suspect that a puzzle fanatic would look with excitement at an empty table and the fresh start it offers them. Sometimes, we forget the freedom that accompanies possibility. And when it comes to discerning our career interests, this freedom allows us to step into opportunities that complement our unique passions and gifts.

Most college graduates will tell you that they are a vastly different person upon leaving college than when they arrived. College is a time when many of us change or refine our beliefs about a wide array of topics, from faith to politics to purpose. So why do we expect ourselves to know exactly which job will align with our skills and values before we even get to college?

Remaining open-minded is one of the greatest gifts you can give yourself in college. During this unique season of our lives, keeping an open mind allows us to grow into fuller versions of ourselves and say yes to unexpected opportunities that may come our way.

Upon reflection, I wish someone had given me permission to take a breath, step back from the spreadsheet, and remember that life is a more enriching adventure when we cannot see the ending. This is both frightening and strangely comforting. Imagine the delight we can experience as we sort through the various puzzle pieces, each with a unique image printed on them. Just as there are many approaches to building a puzzle that can be both enjoyable and effective, there are also many routes that can lead us into a career we feel equipped for and passionate about.

Experimenting and searching for clues

In her TEDx Talk, "Don't Find a Job, Find a Mission," NPR host and opera singer Celeste Headlee said, "We learn about ourselves through practice, not theory." While it may seem that many of our peers already know "who they are" and "what they want to do," the truth is that most of us are still figuring this out. College gives us ample opportunities to follow Headlee's advice to "make the stakes really low."[1] In this setting, we can explore our interests without the pressure that comes from long-term commitments. I remember taking advantage of group projects, leadership programs, club positions, and research opportunities to "experiment" with work that interested me.

Here are a few examples of what this might look like for you:

- Explore clubs at the club fair or online. Try joining a club not for the purpose of putting it on your resume, but because it offers you a chance to do something you have always been curious about.

- Take note of classes that other students rave about, and consider leaving room in your schedule for interesting courses that may differ from those in your major.

- Carve out one night a week to attend speaker events that catch your eye on a flyer or your school's events calendar.

- If you are particularly enjoying a class, consider asking the professor whether they have any research positions available or would recommend supplementary reading material.

Just as when we are constructing a puzzle, the more uncertain we are at a particular point, the more we need to embrace curiosity, trial runs, and even failure on the path toward greater clarity. Think of this process as "searching for clues" on your journey. What do these clues tell us? Well, they can give us important insights that will ultimately benefit us when we are applying for jobs further down the road.

First, these hands-on experiences can reveal the gifts that we may not have tapped into before. Many of us will find that college offers a much wider array of academic opportunities and extracurricular activities than high school did. Thus, we may discover that we have a talent for something we were unaware of before. For me, this looked like developing my facilitation skills by leading engaging group activities and conversations.

Second, the activities we participate in can also reveal our weaknesses. It is easy to stand on the sidelines and dream about the future work we want to do. It is much harder to step into roles that offer us real-world experience. Whether we are serving on a club executive board, working for real clients in a consulting club, or assisting a professor in research, our weaknesses will emerge. When we understand our current limitations, we can work to improve them or bypass certain jobs in favor of work that more strongly aligns with our skill set.

Third, these immersive learning opportunities can show us what it feels like to do work we love. Pay attention to the activities and topics that bring you the most excitement. Which class assignments are you naturally speaking about with eagerness to your friends over coffee? Which tasks for your internship do you gravitate toward first, perhaps even on your off-hours, because you are so enthusiastic about them? Not only does our passion enrich our personal work experience, but it also creates the best path for meaningful contribution. If you need a reminder of what this looks like, think back to chapter 3 where I shared my experience with research in system dynamics. This experience allowed me to use my newly developed skills to support teams that carried out missions I cared deeply about. What could be better?

And fourth, is there work that brings you a sense of dread every time you think about it? Just as working on a puzzle you don't enjoy can be a miserable experience for you and those you are working alongside, be careful not to commit to work that is more life-draining than life-giving. I know how easy it is to get caught up in the race to achieve our goals, especially when we see classmates and friends seemingly doing so with ease. Maybe you set out a plan for yourself when you began college to pursue a specific career. But no matter the allure of a salary or a position, if the work we are doing does not intrigue us, it will be very difficult to sustain a meaningful contribution over time.

As I looked at the clues I gathered, I noticed that the activities I had performed well in and enjoyed immensely did not all fit within a perfect box. While this worried me at first, I realized it was actually a sign that I was following my unique interests rather than trying to fit a generic mold. Just as puzzle pieces come in different shapes, our interests may vary as well.

The hard truth is we cannot chase every opportunity that captures our attention. But I also do not think we are limited to one narrow path. We have an extraordinary capacity to engage in a diverse array of activities. I am still weaving the thread through the interests I do have, wondering which ones might take a front seat and which may emerge in smaller ways or different seasons of my life. But I know that each one influenced who I am today and how I see the world around me. And that is the mark of a meaningful education.

Internships and the stories we tell

Even before beginning college, I remember learning about the value of internships. I had heard that attaining a coveted internship at a reputable company was the best way to ensure success in the job search process and avoid the post-graduation dreaded status: unemployed. Of course, that pressure only led me to overthink the process. I spent many hours researching internships but hesitated to apply for them. Year after year, I reached the beginning of the summer with very few prospects.

I was disappointed by my inability to acquire an impressive internship, a consequence that was largely the result of fear. Still, I tried to embrace those "unconventional" summers as an opportunity rather than a regret. When I was growing up, my dad always found a way to offer words of wisdom that were both logically sound and deeply comforting. So, when he detected my feelings of frustration around internships, he shared words with me that I have never forgotten: "When you are in a job interview, it's how you tell your story that matters." He reminded me that the internship titles on our resumes are only one aspect of the application. "What's more important," he said, "is our ability to authentically share the journeys we took, even if they looked a little different from most students' experiences."

When you think about telling a story, what comes to mind? I used to think that a story was a series of events that occurred. But as I've been studying stories in the hope of writing a novel, here's what I've learned: a plot is *what* happens; a story is *how* what happens *transforms* the main character.[2] In the case of job interviews, telling a story means sharing how your internships or summer experiences have changed you. This doesn't have to be some big transformation. Maybe you learned valuable skills, adopted a new mindset, met people who left an impression on you, or refined your values. If I were to share my story in a job interview, here's what I would say:

"The summer after my freshman year, I didn't have an internship, but I did get to travel abroad. During my trip, I visited several non-profits and social enterprises, including one that invests in entrepreneurs who are living in extreme poverty. I remember sitting across from a group of women as they shared their experiences of receiving training, saving money together, and starting businesses to support their families. As I listened to their stories, I marveled at the power of entrepreneurship to improve lives. Before this trip, I wrestled with my decision to study business because of the cut throat reputation this major has garnered. But on my trip, I learned that businesses run with integrity can empower individuals to contribute to their communities and families in life-changing ways. I could never fully absorb this lesson from a PowerPoint or textbook.

"The following summer, I interned at a nonprofit in Boston, where I worked with a diverse, multigenerational team devoted to serving and empowering Christian leaders in urban settings. And after my junior year, I interned for my dad's small consulting business where I created his website and discovered strengths that were hidden beneath my perfectionist tendencies: resourcefulness, scrappiness, and grit."

Through all these opportunities, my dad reminded me that I had a story to share. Each experience strengthened my resolve to do purposeful work. I learned that if you care enough about the people you are serving and working alongside, you can find the courage to move through obstacles together. And I realized I thrive in environments that celebrate passion and creativity.

Looking back, I am so thankful that I didn't try to make my classes, activities, and internships "look good on paper." Paper is so flimsy, but memories and moments stick with us. They mold us, shape us, and impress lessons on us that will unfold in surprising ways as we move forward. These experiences matter not because of their external appearance but because of the internal transformation they catalyze.

Viewing our internships as a series of experiences that make up a unique story also reduces our temptation to compare our journey with someone else's. The best stories are not interesting because they conform to a well-established model but because they are distinct. Each one of us has our own path to walk. Instead of letting this realization frighten us, perhaps we can appreciate the unique vantage point we have to see the beauty and possibility that others may miss.

The job application process

When my friend Catherine began the job application process, she had a series of clues to aid her in this important decision. So, she began asking herself the following reflective questions in a process she called "taking stock":

- Which classes were most interesting to me?

- What do I enjoy?

- What don't I enjoy?

- What are the themes and patterns in how I chose to spend my time at college?

- What are my core values?

Though she had entered college with an interest in science, Catherine realized that she did not want to be a physician (first of all, blood makes her squeamish!). She also came to see that working in a lab, which had piqued her curiosity at one point, felt too solitary for her. So, what opportunities could she explore? Well, she loved public health classes. The activities she enjoyed shared the threads of service, community, and interdisciplinary thinking. And two of her core values are empathy and active listening.

When Catherine discovered a position in the field of serious illness communication—which centers on making people feel known and cared for and honoring what matters most to them—she knew it was her dream job. After going through the application process, she was offered a job, which she gladly accepted! She now works within a team of passionate individuals who develop innovative healthcare practices to attentively and compassionately care for patients.

By doing work to enhance the quality of the patient experience in the healthcare system, Catherine's job closely aligns with her interests and values. She wasn't familiar with this job when she entered college. But thankfully, she remained open to new experiences, saying yes to opportunities that genuinely intrigued her. As she looked back on her four years, she was able to thoughtfully discern how those pieces fit together to create a picture she loved.

This is the stage when we begin looking backward at the steps we have taken to get here. Or, in puzzle language, when we see how individual pieces come together to create an image we can start to make out. As you look to the future, don't forget to reflect on what you have discovered about yourself over these last few years.

We do not have to go through this discernment process alone. Just as I enjoyed collaborating with my mom and my brother on the puzzle, inviting others into your career decision can open the door to meaningful connections. When you seek guidance from people who have been in your shoes—or individuals equipped to support you—you gain wisdom and learn a significant lesson: the value of asking for help.

Whether you visit the career center, attend job fairs and networking events, or utilize other resources that your college offers, remember that they are a service, not an obligation. Career counseling services can provide you with a wealth of valuable information, but having too many tools and receiving too much advice at once can be more stress-inducing than calming. Rather than giving in to the pressure to do it all, ask yourself which specific resources feel the most valuable to you right now.

It is normal to feel a bit overwhelmed at this stage. You have never done this before, so give yourself grace. It is okay to move slowly. At this pace, you can thoughtfully engage with the process and remain open to unexpected opportunities that arise. Try not to let the notion of your dream role keep you from exploring other exciting opportunities that grab your attention.

Look for purposeful work

In her TEDx Talk, Headlee urged listeners to let go of their pursuit of the "perfect job" and to instead "find a mission." She said, "The most important thing that leads to job satisfaction is purpose." She then explained the connection between her two seemingly unrelated jobs: broadcast journalist and opera singer. Headlee shared, "The core mission of both of them is exactly the same. In both of those jobs, I'm reaching out to people. I'm communicating with people. I'm inspiring people. I'm moving people using only the power of my voice. So now if I'm asked how I got where I am, I say, 'I found my mission and I forgot about the job title.'"[3]

I love her invitation to consider what is beneath the surface of the work we do rather than fixating on the title. It is easy to forget this advice as we scroll through job titles on LinkedIn or our school's job search database. While our success-oriented culture places such a high value on "noteworthy" jobs, Headlee's appeal to find our mission releases us to search for jobs that will truly satisfy our longing for purposeful work.

What would it look like for you to take her words to heart? How might your remaining time at college and your career search be different if you could let go of your desire to attain the "perfect job" and instead pursue a greater call to "find your mission"? You do not need to answer this question quickly—nor do you need to adhere to this decision for the rest of your life. But I hope it will give you a new lens through which to look at this decision, which often feels so consequential.

Her words also speak to an important factor that we can easily forget when we are just starting out on the career path. While past generations often stayed in a particular job for years, it is much more common for our generation to switch jobs several times over the course of a career. Whether we willingly leave our current role for an exciting opportunity or unexpected circumstances force us into a new position, the best way we can prepare for this transition is to embrace the power of reinvention. Headlee reminds us that we do not have to confine ourselves to a particular job description. Instead, we can adapt our skillset and passions to a new role as we keep our mission in mind.

Embrace your current stage

I know this may all feel overwhelming. I invite you to return to this chapter at various points throughout your career search and read the words written for you at the specific stage you are at. When you find yourself surrounded by students stressing about their future careers, you may be tempted to revert to plotting out the perfect path to your destination. But remember there is a better way—a much more meaningful way.

Take a moment to reflect on the stage you find yourself at right now. Rather than trying to rush ahead, ask yourself what value this stage holds. Maybe you are in a dreaming phase, looking at all the possibilities in front of you and beginning to sort out which appeal most to you. Maybe you are at a decision point and are learning that saying no is just as important as saying yes. May you find peace in whatever season you find yourself. And let the blurriness of the future remind you to fix your eyes on what is crystal clear: the present. The people you are discovering your passions and gifts alongside; the classes and internships that are awakening something new and beautiful inside you; the day-to-day work of placing puzzle pieces on the table, even if you don't yet know where they belong. May you realize that this puzzle is uniquely yours and nobody can discredit the extraordinary dedication you have demonstrated as you continue to show up.

In case nobody has told you lately, I am proud of you. I am so, so proud of you for moving toward the future, even when you can't predict how it will turn out. I am proud of you for dreaming and working, and sometimes even letting go of your plans to step into something better.

This winding road holds meaning. Not because it makes perfect sense, but because we choose to keep walking anyway. Sometimes, we must turn back around to remember how we got here. Sometimes, we must stop so we can be still long enough to admire the subtle notes of beauty beneath all the noise. And sometimes, we must keep moving forward, believing that the clues we uncover, often in surprising ways, will point us closer to clarity than we were before.

CHAPTER 8

SAYING YES TO BETTER

On the Choices We Make

Dear resident,

I remember the night I sat all alone on the ground outside the campus bookstore, my stomach twisting in knots. I was so scared. The black night surrounded me as I leaned against the cold, hard wall and pressed my phone to my ear. Mom's gentle voice came through the speaker, trying to comfort me. I had called her in desperation.

"Mom, I was stressed tonight so I started eating. And I couldn't stop. Now I'm in horrible pain. Why did I do this to myself? I feel so weak."

I wish I could say after that night I had learned my lesson. Unfortunately, this is just one snapshot of a scene that happened over and over again. But most often, I didn't call my mom. I just suffered in silence, completely alone.

But that is not the end of the story.

I remember a different night, a few months later. I wandered around campus with the familiar sensation of emptiness that needed to be filled. But before I could turn to food, I ran into a friend in a dorm lobby. This friend shared heartfelt words of gratitude for a gift I had given him a while back. And in doing so, he reminded me that I could share hope with others, even though I felt so broken.

Then I walked through the dining hall where I encountered another friend. He invited me to sit with him, and we opened up about our current struggles with breathtaking vulnerability. And by the end of the night, I no longer felt that restlessness that could only be quenched with food. Instead, I felt a warmth that comes from being connected to others and knowing that you matter to them.

With hope,
Elizabeth

Saying yes to better

As I think back to those two separate nights that ended so differently, I realize they were not separated by drastically different circumstances. Instead, on that latter evening, I made a series of small decisions away from isolation and shame—and closer to connection and acceptance.

When I was in high school, an adult I admired spoke these simple but significant words about the power of our choices: "When you say no to something, you get to say yes to something better."

This advice may seem obvious and simplistic, but I cannot over-state its value as I faced numerous decisions on my college journey. Whether I was struggling to break free from a harmful pattern of behavior or learning how to prioritize meaningful experiences, I discovered the value of saying yes with intention. And while I did not always put this wisdom into practice, I was always thankful when I did.

When we enter college, many of us experience greater freedom and responsibility. We get to decide how to spend our time and money, what to eat, how to care for our bodies, and who to surround ourselves with. Besides increased autonomy, most of us have more opportunities available to us than we did in high school. I remem-ber being amazed by the number of choices I could make each week. There were countless events to fill my calendar, numerous meals to try at dining halls and local restaurants, and plenty of new friends to spend time with. This is certainly an exciting opportunity, and it opens doors for us that were less accessible during our younger years. But while many of these doors are liberating, some lead to pathways that can do us more harm than good.

In this time of transition, you may have well-intentioned peo-ple in your life, like parents and mentors, who offer precautionary advice regarding what not to do: *Don't drink too much. Don't stay up too late. Don't gain the "freshman 15." Don't wait until the night before your exam to start studying.* While this may be worthwhile advice to listen to, if you are like me, you may resist acting upon it because its delivery is neither empowering nor uplifting. Moreover, this advice can be tough to receive when we are struggling with our relationship with food, alcohol, or a harmful pattern of behavior that leaves us spiraling. **But I have discovered that rather than focusing on what** to say *no* to, it is more effective to accept invitations to say *yes* to something better.

Obstacles to meaningful experiences

In the first seven chapters, I invited you to reconsider your fixation on future success and uncover the gifts available to you right where you are. While shifting our view on what gives our lives meaning is the first step on this journey, it is certainly not the last. Along the way, we must continue to make choices that align with our values, even as we face pushback within and around us. Here are a few potential obstacles to cultivating meaningful experiences in college:

1. **Harmful patterns of behavior:** When life is going well, it is easy to make decisions that we are proud of. But when we face unexpected setbacks, we may deal with intense emotions by turning to coping mechanisms we are ashamed of.

2. **Conflicting desires:** In a world full of enticing opportunities, we may have difficulty choosing what to say yes to.

3. **Peer or cultural pressure:** It can be difficult to discern which choices are best for us when we are easily influenced by the people around us.

In the rest of this chapter, I will dive into these obstacles and share how this "saying yes to better" mindset can empower you in your pursuit of meaningful moments.

Breaking harmful patterns through connection

Ever since middle school, I have had a complicated relationship with food. Like many young people, I turned to food in times of stress. I discovered a sense of temporary satisfaction that provided relief amid life circumstances that were beyond my ability to control. When I entered college, I tried to embrace a healthy lifestyle and found success at first. But as life got busier and crazier, food once again became the medicine I used to manage the symptoms of my stress while only worsening the root cause.

While food brought temporary relief, my unhealthy relationship with it generated a growing sense of shame that I felt the need to hide. Some nights after eating until I felt sick, I promised myself that I would not repeat the same action the next day. But much to my disappointment, I often broke those promises as the memory of sickness and regret faded into the background while my desire for fulfillment grew stronger.

We all have our coping mechanisms—the ways in which we try to numb the pain hidden beneath the surface of our external lives. They won't always be dramatic. But we develop these habits to try to fill areas of our lives that feel empty or bring order to the parts that feel overwhelming. Perhaps for you, this looks like binging television shows, drinking beyond the recommended amount of alcohol, or overspending. The problem with these remedies is that they do not last for very long, nor do they address the root of our pain. Worst of all, the shame we often attach to such coping mechanisms can make our heavy loads feel even heavier.

In college, it is easy to struggle with an addiction or a harmful pattern of behavior in private. Growing up, many of us had family members, friends, or teachers who knew us well enough to detect changes in our behavior. But in college, our increased independence makes it easier to hide the messy parts of our lives.

Upon reflection, I realize just how difficult it was for me to muster up the strength to resist binge eating through sheer willpower. A resource that has helped me understand this struggle is Aundi Kolber's book *Try Softer*. Kolber, an author and therapist, wrote this book to push back against the traditional trope of "try harder." In a video discussing the book's message, Kolber shares, "'Try softer' is a fresh approach that tells us we can try differently, instead of trying harder and white-knuckling our way into success or whatever we believe that to be." This approach can actually make us "much more resilient and effective for the long term."[1]

I love her invitation to "try differently." Sometimes, our difficulty quitting a harmful habit has less to do with our lack of determination and more to do with the shortcomings of our approach. I discovered that the times in which my cravings subsided the most were the evenings I spent with other people. These nights looked like drinking tea with residents, spontaneously running into acquaintances in the dining hall, and goofing around with friends in the library. These experiences of connection were a surprisingly powerful barrier against the relentless torrent of thoughts about food that often arose in the evenings. The joy I experienced laughing with friends, the satisfaction I felt engaging in deep conversations, and the hope I found in loving others as they came to love me were my greatest sources of comfort during that time. When I sought connection, my feelings of stress and isolation lost their hold on me, along with the desire to binge.

If you are struggling with an addiction or a habit you are ashamed of, I am so sorry. I know what it is like to feel helpless. Maybe you have been fighting for so long and you feel like nothing has changed. But friend, you are not alone. And you are still worthy of love.

My sincere hope for you is that you will turn toward community and connection in the times you are most tempted to isolate yourself.

I know this is much easier said than done. But consider that reaching out does not have to look like confessing your greatest struggles and sources of pain. Perhaps a more manageable first step looks like inviting a friend over for a movie night when you feel the stress rise in your chest. Or maybe you could go to the dining hall just to sit around other people and let the laughter of strangers cheer you up, pulling you away from your spiraling thoughts for a moment.

Prioritizing what matters most

This "saying yes to better" mindset was also helpful when I was presented with many options and wanted to prioritize the activities that really mattered to me. When I studied abroad in Sevilla, Spain, I quickly discovered just how enticing the night scene was. The lower drinking age, access to a plethora of bars and clubs, and the relatively laid-back Spanish culture made it very easy to stay out drinking as many nights as you desired. I can recall a few evenings when I stayed out super late and drank more than I probably should have. The next morning, I always felt exhausted and spent the rest of the day recovering.

I remember realizing that although those evenings were fun and exciting, they were not the reason I went to Sevilla. It was my first time visiting Europe, and I was so excited to travel to new countries, form deep relationships, and see beautiful landmarks and landscapes. I wanted to feel healthy and energized for every new experience. And so, I decided to adopt a more moderate approach to enjoying the nightlife.

When I made that decision, I was not judging those who frequented bars and clubs, nor did I choose to abstain from these activities altogether. Rather, I realized my "deepest desires." I first heard this term from pastor and author John Mark Comer, who said, "Our strongest desires are not actually our deepest desires."[2]

During my time in Spain, I learned how to listen to the voices of these deeper desires rather than let my immediate desires steer my decisions. In college, not only do we get to practice reflecting on our desires, but we also get to learn from our mistakes and regrets. When we have so many options available to us, we may not immediately know which decisions will align most strongly with our values. But over time, as we look at the impact of our decisions, we will become better at this discernment process.

We do not make decisions in a vacuum

When you look at the individuals you admire—those who live with purpose, deep care, and attentiveness to others—you will see that the small decisions they make matter. Ask yourself, *What are they saying yes to and what are they saying no to?* As I think about these people in my life, I recall my roommate Zoe, who often went to bed early so she could go on long morning runs. I admired her commitment to her health and her discipline, which enabled her to do what she truly loved. Then there was my friend Anna, who always said yes to driving people to the airport because she genuinely loved serving her friends. If you had heard her enthusiastic response to these requests, you may have thought she was just offered a trip to Italy!

You might also observe the everyday choices of people whose lives you do not want to emulate. I am not saying to approach this practice with an attitude of judgment but instead with a posture of curiosity. The people around us can so easily influence us—both for good and for bad. We may have trouble identifying our deepest desires because they sound more like whispers than shouts, buried underneath the surrounding noise.

E. E. Cummings said, "To be nobody-but-yourself—in a world which is doing its best, night and day, to make you everybody else— means to fight the hardest battle which any human being can fight; and never stop fighting."[3] While these words may sound extreme, they highlight the reality that our decisions may not always make sense to the people around us. It is normal to feel misunderstood as we seek to live out our values and stay firm in our convictions. Each one of us has to set our own priorities. But I also believe we can find companions who are earnestly seeking to "say yes to better" too. When you find friends who share your values, I hope you can encourage one another to keep moving forward on this beautiful and imperfect journey.

Discover meaning through your "yeses"

From the first seven chapters, I hope you have a greater sense of the gratifying opportunities available as you envision the remainder of your college journey. Before moving on to the next section, I invite you to dream about the specific experiences you would like to cultivate. *What traditions do you want to create? What activities do you want to dive into? What shared experiences would be most memorable?*

As you dream, do not just choose experiences based on the expectation that college students "should" enjoy them. Instead, remember that many of our initial beliefs about fulfillment may change over time. Throughout the first seven chapters, I invited you to challenge your initial perceptions of a meaningful life by:

- Trading a preference for milestone moments for an appreciation of ordinary ones

- Redefining "conversations that matter"

- Resisting the temptation to "push through" your classes so you can embrace curiosity, connection, and creativity

- Slowing your hurried pace so you can cherish your present experiences

- Letting go of your desire to prop yourself up and stepping into the joy of living generously

- Laying down your pursuit of "heroic justice" and beginning to do your "little bit of good where you are"

- Releasing your desire for immediate clarity about your future career so you can enjoy the ongoing discovery process

Based on these mindset shifts, I invite you to consider how you may respond to this question: *What experiences will truly make my time at college most fulfilling and abundant—not only for me but also for the people I love?* Then, think of some habits you may need to adjust or remove from your existing routine so you can be fully present for these experiences. Try to be honest with yourself. Is there a strategy you used to cope with stress in high school that is no longer serving you in college? Are you spending time and money trying to win the approval of others? Deep down, do you know that these precious resources are better spent with people who love you as you are?

Keep in mind that this process does not require an "all-or-nothing" approach. If perfection is the goal, we will surely fall short time after time. But it is never too late to ask ourselves what we need to let go of to step into something better. In fact, instead of looking at an entire period of your life as a success or failure, I invite you to ask yourself this question each day when you wake up: *How can I move closer to love and connection today?* I think you will be amazed by the power of small steps to lead us into deeper places of healing and joy than we imagined possible. We do not build a meaningful life just by saying no to harmful things. Rather, our lives begin to blossom with meaning as we make intentional choices to say yes to experiences that align with our deepest desires.

If I could turn back time and sit beside my younger self as she shook with fear that painful night, I would lean over to her and tell her to breathe through the pain. I would promise her that there is relief on the other side of it. This feeling of helplessness does not last forever. And instead of looking inward for strength, she can make small choices to reach out to people who care about her. She doesn't have to do it alone. Then I would tell her these words that I want you to know deep in your heart: *The beautiful really is closer than you think. You just have to step outside your room and your own story for a little while, and then you will find it.*

> Note: *If you are dealing with alcoholism, an eating disorder, or something that feels too heavy to carry on your own, ask for help. Seek counseling, talk to an RA, or find a friend to confide in. This mindset didn't always work for me, nor is it a substitute for professional help. But it often did help me when I was feeling "stuck," and I sincerely hope it will offer a reprieve for you as well.*

PART 2

DISCOVER HOPE

SEARCH FOR GLIMMERS OF LIGHT

I loved to wander my campus at night. There was a peace that fell upon that home of mine, where patches of quiet and calm were stitched into the blanket of darkness. I weaved my way along paved paths, up and down stairs, into libraries, and between buildings. I passed groups of other students headed to study sessions or social gatherings. On those evening walks, there were certainly slices of darkness that I walked through—stretches in the road where I could hardly make out the ground a few feet in front of me.

But looking back, I realize there were many sources of light to illuminate the path for me after the sun had fallen asleep. Lampposts lined the paved walkways. Twinkling lights reflected off residents' windows. Classroom lights shone brightly, revealing students studying or laughing or eating a late-night snack. And when no artificial lights were to be found, the moon and the stars danced overhead, reminding me that I was never without light to guide me home.

When we are walking in the dark, both literally and figuratively, feelings of fear creep up and questions sometimes arise. Will our eyes adjust to the darkness? What if we fall and can't get back up? Will we find our way to the other side of the night? And if we do, will our eyes adjust back to the light, so we can behold the beauty of the sunrise? But in these times, we can look for light to lead us forward. For me, this light looked like hope, and I will share the many forms it took in the pages ahead.

As you prepare to read this next section, ask yourself, *What are the sources of hope in my life that light the way forward when the road is dark?*

Maybe you will relate to the stories I share. Or maybe they will remind you of painful experiences you walked through that, although different from mine, forced you to ask yourself difficult questions too. It is not my aim to try to answer these questions. Instead, my intention is to direct your gaze to the sources of light you can turn to when you start to stumble in the darkness.

There is a time up ahead when the sun will rise on the horizon and cover the whole sky with light. But until that day arrives, maybe we can discover small glimmers of light to guide us in the dark. These glimmers are all around us, sometimes in the most unexpected places. We just have to be on the lookout for them. Come now, let us walk this darkened path hand in hand. And let us search for the light together.

CHAPTER 9

BITTERSWEET DONUTS

On Finding Support During Loss

Dear resident,

On the evening before my 19th birthday, I sat outside a Puerto Rican elementary school, watching the sun duck behind the mountains in the distance. It was six months after the catastrophe of Hurricane Maria. A group from my church was spending spring break serving with a local church in San Juan. That evening, we led a Zumba class for children and a church service for adults in the community. When the event concluded, families walked back to their cars in the parking lot and my friends piled into our van. But my mind was over 3,500 miles away.

I held my phone to my ear as layers of sadness and exhaustion washed over me, gluing me to the curb. Dad's voice was somber as he told me my family was seated beside Grammy in her California assisted-living facility. I pictured them holding her hand as she prepared to breathe her final breaths. Although she was unresponsive, my dad held the phone to her ear so I could whisper my goodbye. My voice choked as I tried to find the words to express just what she meant to me. But I quickly realized there would never be enough words. So instead, I shared a memory.

I reminded her of the many evenings she would stand in her kitchen making macaroni and cheese when I was a child. As my brother and I waited in eager anticipation, she mixed stringy mozzarella cheese into the pot on her stove. When she placed our dishes before us, we dug in with our bare hands, a custom only reserved for dinners at Grammy's house. Though she grew up in a well-mannered household, on these nights, her love for us surpassed her appreciation for proper etiquette.

Sitting on that curb so many years later and so many miles away, I thanked her for these special memories. Then I told her I loved her.

The following morning, I awoke early to see a missed call from Dad. My breath caught in my throat as I quietly treaded downstairs in my soft, pink plaid pajamas and slid open the side door. I walked behind the house so I could have a moment of privacy as I returned his call. Leaning against the outside wall, I wiped my tears that flowed freely as he confirmed Grammy had entered heaven that morning.

When I regained my composure, I walked back inside and sat at the glass kitchen table, where I shared the news with a friend. Just a few minutes later, the rest of my friends came downstairs. When I look back at videos from that day, here is what I see: On the table sits a glazed chocolate donut, light flickering from a red candle, and a Krispy Kreme donut hat. As my friends stand around the kitchen in their pajamas singing "Feliz Cumpleaños" to me, I smile politely. But even with my best attempts to appear stoic, you can still see the tears glistening in my eyes behind my narrow rectangular-shaped glasses.

With sorrow,
Elizabeth

The unique challenge of grieving in college

The morning I lost Grammy, I felt like I had whiplash. It was a strange juxtaposition: learning that one of my favorite people in the world was no longer in it, then watching my friends' smiling faces as they greeted me in song. While the experience certainly felt bizarre, I now recognize the blessing of being surrounded by people who loved me when I grieved this hard loss.

If you are grieving today, my heart aches for you. I am so sorry you are hurting. I am so sorry that you have to live with a chasm that feels too wide to fit inside a human heart. I am so sorry that you have to navigate loss when your peers are enjoying tailgates, social events, and campus activities. It seems unfair because it is. Death is deeply unfair. I know the fear that arises when your heart breaks—that hope will remain far away in times like this; that you will look at the same world you have inhabited for many years and suddenly, it will appear upside down.

Grieving in college can be especially tough because we must navigate the everyday stressors of college life on top of the heavy emotions tied to loss. Those of us who attend school far from home might experience an additional layer of loneliness when we feel we are mourning in solitude. Many of us long to be with family who can comfort us in a unique way.

Even if we spend some time with family, returning to college can be hard. You may be tempted to isolate yourself in your grief. When I was younger, I often suppressed my emotions when I was in pain. It felt easier to hold them close to me, not letting others see how much I was hurting. I struggled to share the burdens of grief and despair with those around me when I couldn't understand them myself.

But my experience from that March day of my freshman year challenged my previous inclination to carry my burdens alone. I know that the grieving process can be messy, especially as we struggle to fully articulate our feelings to the ones we love. **But I sincerely believe that leaning on a supportive community is one of the most important steps we can take when we face loss.**

You don't have to carry the burden alone

On the day Grammy passed, I experienced a range of emotions: growing weariness, an ache of sadness, deep gratitude, and great love. While these emotions varied, they all shared this quality: they were raw. I would normally try to hide these intense feelings, but living in such close quarters with my friends prevented me from isolating myself in my grief. As a result, I experienced a surprising sense of freedom. You see, there is something powerful about welcoming unpolished emotions in times of grief. These emotions invite us to be honest with ourselves and the community we are leaning on for support.

You may hesitate to grieve openly because you don't want to become a spectacle. Loss can put a spotlight on us. Pain often draws people to the source—people who genuinely care and want to extend us compassion. But sometimes we feel like they are paying close attention to our reactions, and we must tread carefully under their watchful eyes.

I certainly understand this concern. I am not asking you to walk around like an open book, telling all your classmates and members of your dorm about your loss. But if you have a few trusted friends, I invite you to reach out to them. Let your guard down for a little while. Hear them when they give you permission to cry. Believe them when they say you don't have to carry this weight in private. You might think that your friends just want you to be happy, and you feel guilty for "bringing down the mood." But more than anything, our loved ones want us to feel safe expressing our emotions honestly, especially when we are grieving.

When I was mourning, I was grateful that I did not need to filter my emotions with my friends. Instead, they kindly created space for me to feel whatever I needed to feel in the moment. I felt sad during prayer time. I felt joy when we visited a beautiful waterfall. And I felt grateful at varying times throughout the day when I recalled a special memory with Grammy.

The people who showed up for me on that hard day taught me we do not have to understand someone else's grief to love them. I hope to take this lesson with me in the future. Whether I am being consoled in my own loss or consoling a friend, I hope I can remember that love shows up. My dear friends from that trip expressed this love for me in their own ways: some hugged me, some listened patiently, some laughed with me, and some just included me in perfectly ordinary conversations about that day's activities. But each one comforted me and lessened my feelings of loneliness.

If you are grieving at college, I recognize that your experience may look different from mine. Perhaps you are a part of a close-knit community that is offering you practical and emotional support. Or maybe you are just beginning to settle into your daily routine at college, and your friendships are in the early stages of development. It is understandable if you are hesitant to open up to new friends about your grief. If this is the case, I invite you to find a trusted mentor who can point you to grief resources. This might be your resident director, RA, advisor, or a professor you trust. You do not have to go through this alone.

When you need to be alone

On the flip side, you may long to find spaces to mourn in private. This makes sense given how crowded the college environment can be. As I think back to my return to campus, I recall a morning I spent alone in Eagle's Nest dining hall remembering Grammy. Because most students were still gone for spring break, I felt free to grieve openly. It was cathartic to listen to music while I cried and looked at photos of her over the last 19 years.

We all mourn in our own ways. These ways may vary from day to day as you navigate the grieving process. In the early stages of grief, it may be helpful to carve out periods in your schedule to be alone and honor the person you are mourning. Use this time to reflect on your favorite memories of them. If you enjoy journaling, write your honest emotions, even if they feel complicated (you can always throw the pages away later if you don't want to keep them). Maybe you need to get away from campus. Go on long walks and try to immerse yourself in nature if possible. The slow rhythms of nature offer us a unique space to mourn that we can't find in man-made settings. As you grieve, I hope you can really listen to what your mind, body, and soul need. Instead of turning to harmful coping mechanisms to just "get through" this hard season, take the time and space you need to seek genuine sources of comfort.

Of course, carving out time to mourn is not the same as compartmentalizing your feelings. Your grief will probably affect many areas of your life, maybe even in unexpected ways. Don't give in to the lie that you must move at the same pace you did before the loss. My therapist once told me that grief can be exhausting. It is normal to be tired and need more time to perform your daily activities. Be gentle with yourself—and let the people around you support you when you feel like you are falling apart.

When unpleasant emotions arise, our first inclination is often to ignore our feelings and try to rush back to "normal." Sitting in our sadness can feel uncomfortable. But there is value in slowing down so we can face the pain. I know it may seem counterintuitive—that we must begin by sitting with *what is* before we can move forward. But I think it is one of the truest things I know about grief: we must greet it when it comes to us.

Welcome the bittersweet

Grief has taught me a lot about the messiness of life. In the college culture, it is especially easy to fall into an "all-or-nothing thinking" mindset. I often defined a day as "good" or "bad." I judged classes, activities, and opportunities with a similar binary lens. But life is seldom that simple. And rather than resent the complexity of life, I am learning to find the grace in it—for even in my deepest pain, I am still capable of receiving good gifts.

In her book *Bittersweet*, writer and lecturer Susan Cain shares these words: "We're built to live simultaneously in love and loss, bitter and sweet."[1] On the day we lost Grammy, it surprised me how quickly I embodied both states of being at once. I suppose the stark contrast between mourning a loss and celebrating a birthday magnified this powerful experience. But I think most of us experience it to some degree in the grieving process.

What does it look like to mourn with a "bittersweet" disposition? I think it is fairly easy to recognize the "bitter" that accompanies loss. No matter the age of our loved one or the circumstance of their passing, we always wish we could have a bit more time with them, don't we? Even though we have scientific explanations for life on Earth, death will always be a mystery. If loving someone enough could keep them here, we would hold on to them forever.

And what about the "sweet"? This doesn't always come right away. But over time, many of us will feel immense gratitude for the life of our beloved. We will recall the supreme sweetness of loving and being loved. Although they are no longer with us, we will carry so much of their light with us. I know I will carry Grammy's appreciation for beauty, her generosity, her deep faith in Jesus, and her ability to see the belovedness in everyone she encountered.

Francis Weller, a psychotherapist who specializes in grief, shared this reflection on the dual nature of our grief: "The work of the mature person is to carry grief in one hand and gratitude in the other and to be stretched large by them. How much sorrow can I hold? That's how much gratitude I can give. If I carry only grief, I'll bend toward cynicism and despair. If I have only gratitude, I'll become saccharine and won't develop much compassion for other people's suffering. Grief keeps the heart fluid and soft, which helps make compassion possible."[2]

May you find peace

When someone loses a loved one, it is common for us to share our condolences with words to this effect: "May you find peace." Growing up, I had little understanding of what that actually meant. What is the value of peace? And how do we find it?

I suppose I spent much of my life chasing feelings of happiness. And then in seasons of loss and pain, I often sought answers or relief. But as I grow older, becoming more familiar with my own grief and the grief of loved ones, I see just how powerful peace is.

Peace and sadness are not incompatible. On the day of Grammy's passing, I got a small glimpse of the peace that would take many months to fully settle upon me. I was swimming in the ocean when I drifted a short distance from my friends. I lay on my back and let the waves buoy me gently up and down. As I gazed at the blue sky above me, my eyes filled with tears. But the sadness was not entangled with fear. Instead, I had a sense of peace about it. It was as if this peace invited me to accept sorrow as a fact of life. I think part of growing up is acknowledging these emotions when they arrive, no matter how unpleasant, and understanding that they will not last forever. Perhaps the path to peace begins when we stop fighting our powerful emotions and start feeling them.

I don't think peace is something we can arrive at with a five-step self-help plan. It looks different for each one of us. Some of us may receive it in small doses that add up over time, like drops of water we collect in a bottle. Or it may wash over us in one powerful moment, like a wave that cleanses us of sticky sand and invites us forward with a renewed lightness. Peace is not always logical. It is felt in our hearts, not deduced with our brains.

May you find people who can point you toward peace—not

platitudes or emotionally detached analysis. People who understand that grieving is a sacred process. One that can be walked alongside but never raced ahead. One that gives us a remarkable glimpse into the depths of our humanity. Brazilian novelist Paulo Coelho said, "Only two things can reveal life's great secrets: suffering and love."[3] Perhaps this experience of grief invites us to discover the secrets revealed in suffering and love all at once. And while this journey can take us to tender places, the people who walk with us remind us we do not have to discover these secrets alone.

CHAPTER 10

CLEANING PAINT IN "66"

On Asking for Help

Dear resident,

After a laughter-filled paint night with friends, I walked with paint-stained hands, plastic palettes, and brushes down to the basement of "66," one of BC's sophomore dorms. My friend Kristin held the door open as I walked into the small public restroom. After the heavy door slammed behind us, we began to clean off the paint with paper towels.

I can't remember how long we were there or what I asked Kristin. But I do remember her leaning against the sink, starting to open up about a struggle with anxiety she had been experiencing in recent months. As she reflected on the heavy burden she was carrying—this weight that felt crippling at times—I was surprised. I had no idea she was dealing with this despite the many moments we had spent together that year. My heart swelled with compassion as she described the constant pressure on her chest, which made it difficult for her to take a full breath.

There was a mirror in that little bathroom, and as I think back to that moment, it was as if Kristin was holding up a mirror to me. As I listened to her speak, I felt like she was saying all the words out loud that I had been playing in my head over and over. And in that moment, I knew I was not alone.

When she finished sharing, I told her about the past few months of my life—and the days that rolled into weeks when I felt a pressure building inside me with no outlet. During that time, I felt burdened by some of my own stressors and the painful experiences of people who confided in me. I now realize that I struggled with emotional regulation and healthy compartmentalization, tools that I would develop in the following years through therapy.

We stood in that room for a long time, relieved to release some of the tension that had been filling our chests. I remember thinking how peculiar it was to be huddled in a tiny bathroom in the basement of a college dorm on a Saturday night, as people likely circled above and around us, dancing or drinking their cares away. But although it was small and dark, it felt more safe than scary. It was like a haven where we could retreat from the chaos. Being hidden from the world gave us both space to confess our fears and our questions—and to find hope in the realization that we were not alone.

In solidarity,
Elizabeth

The lies that keep us stuck

If you are struggling with your mental health in college, I am sorry. As I sit here several years after that spring of my sophomore year, reading journal entries filled with such heavy emotions, I know that anxiety is not something to be taken lightly. Whether you have a diagnosed mental health condition or you are walking through a season of poor mental health, I know it is difficult to navigate this confusing terrain in an already stress-filled college environment.

If this is not a challenge you can relate to, there is a good chance someone close to you can. According to the 2022-2023 Healthy Minds Survey, which collected responses from undergraduate and graduate college students, 44% reported symptoms of depression, 36% of anxiety disorder, and 14% of suicidal ideation.[1] I hope this chapter will give you a greater understanding of the reality that many people with mental health conditions face so you can support a loved one through this difficult experience.

As I think back to that spring of my sophomore year, I remember it not only for the heaviness I carried around in my chest but also for conversations like the one I had with Kristin. Each time I was able to be honest about my experience of anxiety, I felt a little less frightened of it. Bringing the truth into the light was like poking a balloon with a pin and watching it slowly deflate. Speaking up and reaching out for help was a decision I am immensely proud of. But the courage it took did not come quickly.

There were several lies I believed that held me back from seek-ing help for a long time. In this chapter, I will examine each of those lies and share the truths I have come to believe instead. I now realize how easily we can believe these lies when we are in a fragile emotional state. **It is in the moments when we need the most support that our minds often trick us into believing we are not worthy of receiving it.**

These are the three lies:

- Lie #1: I am the only one.
- Lie #2: Needing help makes us weak.
- Lie #3: Asking for help must be a dramatic declaration.

Lie #1: I am the only one

When I was in high school, I worked hard to conceal that I was struggling through a season of depression. I spent a lot of time and energy pretending I was happy, even though I was experiencing intense sadness. While I eventually had some honest conversations with loved ones, most of the time I suffered in silence. Experiencing a condition like anxiety or depression can be overwhelming in and of itself. But when you add the fear that nobody will understand you, you may feel even more isolated.

In the years since high school, I have talked to several friends who were walking through similar situations. In hindsight, I real-ize just how wrong my assumption was that this pain was unique to me. But at the time, it felt impossible to see beyond the happy faces that other people wore.

If I could go back in time and tell my high school self one thing, it would be this: You know that friend who looks so happy? The one you are often jealous of because she seems to navigate life with such ease? You know your belief that she would never understand your overwhelming sadness or the panic that comes out of nowhere? Well, there is a good chance that she understands more than you think. There is a good chance that she believes these same things about you. In fact, so many of your classmates are carrying invisible burdens that they have spent years learning to conceal.

This realization leads me to wonder—how would I treat my classmates differently if I found out they too had a panic attack the night before the exam? Is it possible that my friend who always looks put together wrestles with the same loneliness and insecurity that I do? What if my loneliness no longer has to be something I carry in secret, filling me with shame? What if I could take these broken pieces of my story and let them build a bridge of compassion that I can cross to move toward others in love?

I don't know what weights you are carrying. I don't know what thoughts circle through your head as you eat ice cream around a crowded table of smiling faces or paint pretty colors on a canvas with the people who you love most at college. But I do know that one of the most dangerous things we can do when we are in pain is look at everyone else's smiles and tell ourselves that they couldn't possibly understand. That we are alone in feeling this way—anxious and afraid. The harmful effects of this assumption are two fold: We hurt ourselves when we believe the lie that we have to suffer alone, and we are less generous with our compassion when we convince ourselves that the people around us don't need it.

Lie #2: Needing help makes us weak

From a young age, many of us were told—implicitly or explicitly—that a strong, successful person works through challenges on their own. If you don't know the answer, pretend you do. If you are insecure or lonely, hide it. If you are uncertain about the future, create a five-year plan and follow it closely. And to a large extent, this is what we've done. We've embraced the gospel of self-reliance with enthusiasm, believing that the pressure we put on ourselves will be worth it in the end.

But what happens when we really do need help? When the load we are carrying suddenly becomes heavier and our knees start to buckle underneath its weight? When our physical wellbeing starts to suffer from the emotional turmoil spinning inside us, like a washing machine that shakes when it is filled to the brim?

When will we give ourselves permission to be human? To realize it is not only okay—but actually a good thing—to speak up when the burden we are carrying is starting to overwhelm us? To admit that we still need hard-won wisdom from people who have walked this road ahead of us? And to seek help from professionals who remind us we don't have to settle for just surviving?

It is tempting to run away from the versions of ourselves we are less proud of. Trust me, I've been there. But what if it is not our weakness that we should be ashamed of? Instead, what if the real enemy is a society that pressures young people to project an image of confidence, even when they are hurting underneath? What if the culprit is a culture that glorifies individualism, even though humans were created to depend on each other?

When we are so afraid of looking weak, we miss out on the chance to discover how strong we really are. For a long time, I thought that being strong meant "not needing help." But I now know what a limited definition that is. Think about the strength you have mustered in moments of vulnerability. That was anything but weakness. It takes a unique kind of strength to unclench our fists, hold open our palms, and say, "I have nothing left. I am worn out and lost. I need help."

Lie #3: Asking for help must be a dramatic declaration

I am the kind of person who spends a lot of time anticipating a difficult conversation before I have it. In fact, my fear of such conversations often causes me greater distress than the conversation itself.

I certainly wasn't looking forward to calling my parents from college and telling them that I was having spiraling thoughts and uncontrollable fears. I liked being their independent, capable, optimistic daughter. *What would they think of me when they heard how often I was catastrophizing? Would they become worried about my wellbeing? Would they overreact, causing me to feel even more afraid of my own mind?*

But when I finally did call them, I was surprised by their response. They didn't sound frightened. They didn't make me feel crazy. They met me with compassion. They reminded me I was loved. And then, we calmly talked about finding a therapist who I could meet with to work through the distress I was experiencing.

When we believe there is only one way to ask for help—and we imagine it looking like a big confession received with shocked expressions—no wonder we are afraid to speak up. But what if we could be gentler with ourselves? What if there are many ways to ask for help?

Sometimes, the first step is being honest with ourselves. Maybe it means writing your emotions and thoughts in a journal. Seeing them all in one place can help you more objectively recognize patterns in your thinking.

Or perhaps you will begin by sharing your experience with a friend in a moment of vulnerability, like I did with Kristin. I didn't plan to open up to her, but after she bravely shared her experience with me, I felt safe to do the same. Oftentimes, when someone asks us how we are doing, we respond with the generic response, "I'm fine." But what might it look like to just open the door a crack? You don't have to swing it wide open, but you could show a glimpse of the mess. Consider saying, "Actually, I've been feeling pretty anxious lately." Or "These last few months have felt overwhelming. Do you think we could go to coffee so I can process these big emotions?" You do not have to be flippant with this decision. It is wise to be deliberate about who we are inviting into this sacred space. But I am learning that if I live in constant fear of vulnerability, refusing to open up even to the most trustworthy, grace-filled friends, then I miss out on the opportunity to find hope through another person's compassion and encouragement. What a loss that is.

In addition to trusted friends, sometimes we need professional help. After serving as an RA, I know firsthand the systems put in place to support students with a broad range of mental health concerns. While these systems are far from perfect, I do believe they are made up of people who genuinely care about our wellbeing. You may be hesitant to take advantage of these services because you want to handle your problem on your own. After all, college is a wonderful time to take on new responsibilities and learn practical skills without relying on your parents (cooking, laundry, grocery shopping, etc.). But when it comes to mental health, the same rules do not apply. Please don't try to prove that you can push through the pain by yourself when your mind is suffering. No matter how old we get, there is no shame in asking for help.

Whether you are seeking support for yourself or a friend, it is helpful to remember that there are a range of emotional states we may find ourselves in. Sometimes, we are in search of tools to cope with uncomfortable thoughts and emotions before they progress further. Other times, we are experiencing acute psychological distress and feel desperate. Here are some practical steps you can take in each scenario:

Finding help proactively:

- If you are experiencing psychological symptoms that you are struggling to cope with on your own, schedule an initial consultation through your school's counseling services.

- If you feel comfortable involving a parent or guardian, set up a meeting to discuss how they can support you in finding a mental health professional to work with.

- Put the following phone numbers in your phone at the beginning of the school year so you have access to them in case of an emergency.

Finding help in a crisis:

- Call your RA, the on-call RA, or your resident director.

- Your university counseling services website will likely have a number you can call to speak to an emergency clinician.

- Call your campus police or 911.

- Suicide and Crisis Lifeline: Text or call 988.[2]

You are more than your pain

Many years have passed since I began to confront the reality that my mind doesn't always work the way I would like it to. I am now very open with others about the power of therapy and medication on my healing journey. And I have found many friends and acquaintances who I am able to relate to and encourage.

While I no longer feel so restrained by the lies I shared with you earlier, I still find myself wrestling with other misbeliefs about how my mental health affects my identity. So, this is what I need you to know: I am more than my pain. You are more than your pain. We are more than our pain.

Maybe you are right in the middle of it, and it feels all-encompassing. Maybe you have been receiving treatment for years, and it feels more like a nagging sensation that you can never fully shake. However big or small it feels right now, remember that it is *not everything*. Your life may be affected by a diagnosis or a difficult period of emotional turmoil, but this does not inform your identity. It does not decide who you are.

When I was going through an especially distressing period after graduating, it was so important to remind myself of this. I pursued projects that I was passionate about—a reminder of how creative my mind is. I found meaningful ways to serve neighbors and loved ones—a reminder that I wasn't just in need of help but could contribute to other people's lives too. I was intentional about having fun, lighthearted experiences—a reminder that life does not have to be serious all the time. And above all, I leaned on friends to remind me just how wonderfully complex my life is—a life that can never be reduced to a diagnosis or a moment of weakness.

CHAPTER 11

THE SUMMER BEFORE SPAIN

On Caring vs. Carrying

Dear resident,

"There is just so much pain in the world. And I don't know what to do with it."

I remember the desperation in my voice. I remember the feeling of hopelessness that weighed my body down.

My therapist looked up at me from her notepad, a gentleness emanating from her deep blue eyes. She had a thoughtful look on her face. I could tell that she was searching for the right thing to say. She knew that I didn't want easy answers or platitudes.

"What if we begin with the people closest to you? A roommate who needs a ride to work; a friend who is grieving. How can you support them? How have you already shown up to love them in their pain?"

I suppose her words weren't groundbreaking, but they were exactly what I needed to hear. As we began identifying specific people in my life who I could help in tangible ways, I felt a renewed sense of purpose. This elusive "pain in the world" suddenly morphed into something more tangible. There was a freedom that accompanied this realization: I wasn't called to save the world—only to love the people right in front of me.

I had entered therapy that summer feeling like I had the weight of the world on my shoulders. My mind raced with fears about my fate and the wellbeing of my loved ones. I imagined tragedies in my head on a loop from stories I read about in the news or heard in random conversations. But I wasn't just imagining the events that happened to others; I was imagining the pain they felt.

As we worked together to address this "over-empathizing," as I had come to call it, we discussed two harmful tendencies I was prone to: catastrophizing about the future and soaking in the pain of others like a sponge—feeling responsible for burdens that were not mine to carry. With a compassionate spirit, my therapist reminded me that this practice of ruminating on unlikely circumstances robbed me of the hope I needed to move through very real challenges. She also helped me to acknowledge the cost of trying to carry the pain of everyone around me: the destruction of my own sense of peace. It took many hard days and nights, but I began to approach the pain of those around me from a new perspective. I came to see that I could love people without letting their pain break me.

With grace,
Elizabeth

Caring isn't the problem

It is hard to live in a world where pain writes itself not only on the pages of our stories but also on our loved one's stories. If you are struggling to experience joy where you are because you have a keen understanding that the world is deeply flawed and seemingly broken beyond repair, you are not alone. If you are struggling to find hope when you watch the news or walk alongside friends during painful seasons, you are not broken. You are human.

I used to think caring was the thing that would break you—until I realized how wrong I was. Caring is not the problem. It is carrying burdens for longer than we should. It is letting our thoughts spiral—not just about our own lives, but about the endless list of dangers that could befall the people we love. And it is believing that we are superheroes put here to save them from the pain we did not cause but feel we must alleviate somehow.

When we release the responsibility of carrying other people's burdens, we are free to care deeply for them. And isn't that what we want? Deep down, don't we want to show up with compassion for our hurting friends and remind them that they are not alone when everything falls apart? This is a beautiful desire.

As I write these words today, I believe they are not just valuable for my younger self. They are valuable for each of us who believes that to love people well, we must feel their emotions to the point of ceaseless empathy.

Strong but delicate

As I think about the many tender hearted people I know and love, I connect with them over our ability to experience strong emotions. While this gift draws us toward people with a unique level of compassion and empathy, it also means that we need to protect our hearts and minds. Recognizing that this attribute is a double-edged sword is the first step toward simultaneously caring for ourselves and those we love.

In my search for a metaphor to explain this strange experience of walking around with what feels like both a gift and a curse, I looked up "objects that are strong but delicate" and came across "Prince Rupert's drop." I watched a video of a man displaying a glass bead with a thick ball at the end and a very thin tail that juts outward. He tried to crush the droplet with a hammer, and he hit it hard, but it did not budge. Then, with a slight movement of the tail, he caused the whole object to explode.[1]

It got me thinking about how strong the human heart is. We can endure loss, fear, disappointment, and heartache, developing resilience that allows us to move forward with hope. I look back amazed at the hard situations I have overcome in my life when I had no other choice but to push through them. And yet, if we put undue stress on our hearts by carrying loads that are not ours to carry, we may be left shattered. Perhaps this will not happen in an instant like with Prince Rupert's drop. But over time, if we continue to carry the heartbreak, suffering, and burdens of people around us without learning how to release them in healthy ways, the effects may be detrimental. We won't feel valiant or heroic at all. Caring won't feel like a gift, and love won't feel like a gentle invitation to connect. It will all feel heavy. It will all look bleak.

Can you relate to this experience? Consider the ways that your love for a friend or family member may have caused you to worry excessively. How did this affect your ability to move through your own life with a sense of peace? Here are a few ways it manifested in my life:

- I struggled to take care of myself in basic ways like eating healthy and keeping my house tidy.

- I was unable to actually sit with a hurting person in their pain or offer practical support in a time of need.

- I catastrophized about future events in my sphere of influence and the world at large.

- I fixated on the sadness, grief, and bitterness around me while my appreciation of the many beautiful aspects of life faded.

You can see how stuck I felt in that heavy-laden season. I struggled to remain hopeful that life would get better for people I knew who were hurting. While I often imagined the pain of others, going so far as to feel their emotions in my mind and body, I could not experience the relief of healing. You can't heal from a wound that was never yours to carry.

Reimagining empathy

If I had to articulate the belief that directed many of my actions during that season, it would be this: *To love people well, we must feel each of their emotions and absorb their pain through empathetic osmosis.* Let us hold this belief up to the light. When you read these words, what comes to mind? Do they feel true? Do they fill you with a sense of unease? Is it possible that they are incomplete—or take something beautiful, like *compassion*, and stretch it to an extreme degree?

If I were to reimagine how I could use my gift of empathy, I would begin with the length of time I spend ruminating on my concern for a friend. The source of my inclination to ruminate is two-fold: my genuine concern leads me to worry, and my love for my friend makes me feel guilty for enjoying my day when I know they are in pain. The problem with this tendency is that it does more harm than good. In fact, I do not actually feel overwhelmed when I sit with a hurting friend. Instead, the distress arises when I let my mind spiral throughout the day, imagining the emotional turmoil that accompanies my friend's grief, fear, or betrayal. It occurs on long drives when I replay heavy conversations and feel physical tension rise in my body.

Henry David Thoreau said, "Could a greater miracle take place than for us to look through each other's eyes for an instant?"[2] How beautiful. I hope you will experience the privilege of caring deeply for your friend as they share a past hurt, a current struggle, or anxieties about the future. Maybe you will receive them with whole-hearted empathy for a moment. But Thoreau does not say that this exchange should last forever. He does not exhort us to walk through entire seasons of our lives with another person's eyes while our own eyesight goes blind. Ultimately, we must embody our own emotions before we can empathize with somebody else's.

A second way we can reimagine empathy is by reevaluating our role as we accompany people through life. Instead of overidentifying as "helpers," we can adopt a posture of "being with" others in times of sorrow *and* joy. Although being honest with ourselves, especially about the very tender places in our stories, can be hard, I believe that it can open the door to healing. So here is my confession: In my sincere attempts to love the people in my life who were struggling, I often unwittingly made their pain about me. If reading these words stings a little, it may be because you have done this too. I think that this tendency actually comes from a very well-meaning place. We see a world that appears apathetic to suffering, especially the suffering of those in vulnerable situations. And so, we start to derive our value from our ability to show compassion to hurting people.

I recognized this mindset in myself, along with its consequences, when I listened to an interview with Father Gregory Boyle, a priest who runs a ministry for former gang members in Los Angeles. If anyone has experience showing up for people in their pain day after day, it is him. Boyle reflected, "The only reason people burn out is not because of compassion fatigue, but it's because they've allowed it to become about themselves. And they have sort of inadvertently insisted that somehow, you know, it's their job to fix and save and rescue. But if you insist that it not be about you, then what you're doing is you're delighting in the people in front of you, and you're receiving people and you're allowing your heart to be altered. And that's eternally replenishing. You won't ever be depleted if you do that."³

What if our gift of empathy was not just a pathway to compassion but also an invitation to joy? When we are "delighting in the people in front of [us]," we get to experience their joy and celebration, not just their sorrows. And we see *who they are*, not just the bad things that happened to them. It is dangerous to look at one page of someone's life and assume that we know the whole story. And it is unfair to see the people around us solely for what they have lost in the storms of life and not the courage they have mustered to rebuild from the rubble. When we make it our goal to see the *whole* person before us, we are less likely to oversimplify their story and overidentify ourselves as their "rescuers."

Setting boundaries to protect our peace

I don't know what burdens you are walking alongside today. Perhaps a friend has just learned of a difficult diagnosis in their family or experienced a tragic loss they are struggling to cope with. Maybe your friend has opened up about an addiction they are facing or the broken heart they are nursing, and you wonder if they will ever feel whole again.

We are at a loss when these things happen, aren't we? Being on the periphery of pain does not exempt us from feeling the sting of it. But if we truly want to show up for our hurting friends, we must create a plan to support others without sacrificing our own wellbeing. The beauty of this balance is that we are better equipped to care for our friends when we are in a peaceful state. I would like to share two practical parameters, or boundaries, that have protected my sense of safety while also enabling me to remain attentive to others.

The first parameter is helpful when we are ruminating on our loved ones' burdens. If you find yourself doing this, ask yourself: *Is excessively thinking about my friend's troubling situation contributing to my ability to care for them well? Or is it draining my capacity to be encouraging when I am present with them?* If your answer is the latter, give yourself permission to shift your thoughts to your other responsibilities. Carrying on with your day the best that you can, even while your heart is breaking for your friend, does not mean you don't love her immensely. It just means you are holding space for her in your heart while recognizing you are not the main character in her story of pain. You can play a supporting role. You can grieve with her. But ultimately, you cannot grieve for her.

The second parameter is based on a model from Stephen Covey's popular book *The 7 Habits of Highly Effective People*. Covey distinguishes between two spheres that our cares fall into: our circle of influence (things that we can directly affect) and our circle of concern (things that we may care about but can do very little to change).[4] This model is helpful for sorting out where we want to devote our attention and energy. I try to catch myself when I am fixating on elements outside my circle of influence. Oftentimes, this looks like watching the news excessively or scrolling through social media. While we do not have to completely ignore the elements outside our circle of influence, we must be careful that they don't take over our worries. The more we devote our attention to the elements we can affect, the more empowered we will feel to make a real change in the world around us. Of course, this is not a call to try to control the people within our orbit; instead, we can influence them in positive ways.

Do these strategies sound helpful to you? Are there additional "soft rules" you can implement as you reimagine your relationship with empathy? As we learn to set boundaries, we experience the freedom to love *both* ourselves and our friends well. We are able to show up with generous and capable hands because we are not weighed down to the same degree as those who are in crisis.

What would it look like for you to receive the pain of others, let it inform your perspective and deepen your compassion, then release the burden of ruminating on it? To do this well, you may need to surround yourself with a support system. If you are a person of faith, prayer can be a wonderful way to share these burdens with God and ask Him to comfort the ones you love. Or perhaps you can talk to a therapist, RA, or mentor. Sometimes we just need a verbal outlet to process our own pain and the pain around us that we often feel powerless to alleviate. Loving others in their pain is seldom easy. But it becomes less overwhelming when we let others meet us with compassion, just as we do for our hurting friends. This is the beauty of community. This is how we move forward—never alone, always together.

A newfound lightness

As I think back to my own dark summer, I remember many heavy days when I struggled to drive into the city for my internship or my therapy appointment. I was planning to study abroad in Spain that fall, but truthfully, I wondered how I would ever be well enough to live on my own across the world when any number of factors could go wrong. I could get sick, I could get injured, I could experience terrible homesickness, I could lose a family member and never get the chance to say goodbye.

But here's the beauty of hope: it gives us something to believe in. It gives us eyes to see the future through the lens of possibility instead of loss. It points us toward wonder when our eyes were once bent toward despair. That summer, hope did not come easily to me—nor did it come in one big moment of clarity. Instead, it came in many small instances of bravery and love, which, stacked on top of each other, gave me the boost I needed to see over the walls that had enclosed me. Finally, I could begin making my way to the other side.

Sometimes, this process of discovering hope in our lives requires us to rethink the way we have been processing pain—whether it be our own or someone else's. If we want to move forward with greater peace, we need to make a significant change. It is not easy to admit our need for healing, especially when we have convinced ourselves that our pain is worth the sacrifice if it connects us to others. But wow, the healing is worth it!

On September 1, my brother dropped me off at Boston Logan Airport with a big red duffel bag and a blue backpack that I carried through many adventures in Europe over the next four months. As I walked through those doors, I left behind the remaining weight I had begun the process of shedding that summer, through many tears and difficult conversations. And I was free to greet every beautiful thing that was waiting for me across the ocean.

CHAPTER 12

A RAINY-DAY
MONOLOGUE

On Gaining Perspective

Dear resident,

> "This day is called the feast of Crispian.
> He that outlives this day and comes safe home
> Will stand o' tiptoe when this day is named
> And rouse him at the name of —"[1]

"We can't hear you. Speak up. You're a king!"

My sympathy for my classmate grew as my acting professor's loud voice boomed back at him across the black box theater. He was rehearsing King Henry V's famous speech for our Shakespeare monologue unit as the rest of the class looked on.

A few minutes passed as we watched this simultaneously entertaining and cringe-provoking spectacle. My jovial professor Luke tried his best to evoke enthusiasm fit for a king preparing his soldiers for battle. And to his credit, my classmate's voice rose a little with each encouragement. But despite his earnest efforts, he kept falling short.

This is when Luke took drastic measures.

"Okay, we're going outside. Follow me, everyone."

So, there we went, ten college students on an impromptu "field trip" to wherever Luke believed he could unleash our classmate's confidence.

Wrapped in our warm sweaters and rain jackets, we followed him through the parking lot and across the street, where we stopped on the sidewalk at the base of a seven-story parking garage. We all turned and looked at Luke expectantly. Addressing my classmate, he said, "Now we're going to stand down here, and I want you to deliver your speech from the top of the parking garage." As he ascended the stairs, we began giggling like children. Something about the prospect of this unexpected adventure delighted us.

When he reached the top, he walked toward the railing so we could see him. Despite the distance, the uncertainty on his face was evident. Water began to trickle from the sky, which only heightened the drama of the moment.

At first, he spoke quietly. But after a few more attempts, he began to shout his monologue with greater clarity and a growing sense of urgency. Even with the sound of our laughter, the rain hitting the pavement, and cars passing behind us, we could hear him.

And with one final triumphant shout, he proclaimed:

> "This day shall gentle his condition;
> And gentlemen in England now abed
> Shall think themselves accursed they were not here,
> And hold their manhoods cheap whiles any speaks
> That fought with us upon Saint Crispin's day."[2]

On the sidewalk below, we cheered and clapped for him. We knew he was not really a king. But he sure sounded like one.

Cheerfully,
Elizabeth

The value of perspective

Reflecting on that rainy day of my sophomore year, I know that Luke sent our classmate to a higher location because he wanted him to shout his lines to us. And what better way to encourage him to speak up than to increase the distance his voice needed to travel?

But I also wonder if he needed a change of perspective.

Perhaps he needed to stand far above us to embody the role of a king and deliver his monologue with confidence to his troops below. Perhaps he needed to see the stark contrast between his position high above us and our lowly positions far beneath him to feel the gravity of his power. Perhaps he needed to see himself and the world around him in a new light to show up with the courage that was difficult to find in that small black box theater.

Just as my classmate struggled to convincingly deliver his lines in the classroom, our efforts to address the problems right in front of us can be ineffective when we have the wrong perspective on them. Although my classmate was playing a role, many of us struggle to show up to our very real challenges with courage and a healthy mindset.

As you know by now, I used to cope with stress in unhealthy ways. Whether it was an argument with a friend, an intense week of exams, or an unexpected bout of sickness, I fixated on the immediate problems in front of me. And I was disappointed by how easily I let the weight of my present circumstances cloud my vision of a hopeful future.

As we continue this journey of discovering hope right in the middle of our pain, we know how important it is to remember that our temporary difficulties will not last forever. Understandably, this can be hard to do when we feel the weight of these pressures closing in on us. So, maybe we can take a page out of Luke's book and look beyond the small box we've found ourselves in. **It is okay to step away from our stressors for a little while to get perspective on them. Finding a new angle does not fix our problems, but it does give us space to breathe, reflect, and remember what matters most.**

Change your vantage point

Where do you find yourself today? Are you sitting at your desk in a cramped dorm room ready to throw the calculator across the room where your basket of dirty laundry overflows onto the carpet? Are you panicking in the library because you procrastinated on an important essay that is due soon? Are you sitting in the noisy dining hall replaying a fight with a friend in your mind over and over again?

These circumstances feel so urgent and consequential. Sometimes, we believe that if we stare at a problem hard enough, we can fix it. But deep down, we know that we can't change every situation through sheer willpower. Oftentimes, ruminating on a problem only worsens it. So, how about we try a new approach? Why don't you step away from whatever is overwhelming you for a moment? You may be hesitant to loosen the reins. But trust me, it is worth it. Put down the pen, close your laptop, walk out of the crowded room, and soak in the fresh air. And as we release our grip on control, we can begin searching for hope.

Why is hope so important? Well, life can hit us hard. When this happens, we may feel like a person who turned their back to the ocean for just a moment and gets pummeled by a wave we did not see coming. In the wake of difficult moments, we need a hopeful perspective to help us move forward. This is not a call to dismiss the very real stressors that keep us up at night or invalidate the unpleasant emotions that arise as we navigate through this beautiful and broken life. Instead, it is an invitation to expand our vantage point.

Imagine we could meet on BC's campus and expand our perspectives together. I would invite you to meet me in one of my favorite places on campus. Located on top of an archway is a walkway that connects two of the school's main academic buildings. Rows of comfortable chairs line the walls on both sides. Between classes, students often settle into the chairs and look through large glass windows onto the green below.

As we peer through one of the windows, we start to see this familiar campus from a new angle. There is something about *embodying* this mindset shift that strengthens its effect. From back here, we can ask ourselves these questions:

- What do we see that we may have missed before?

- What sounds do we hear, and what sounds are too far away
  to hear clearly?

- What thoughts come to the forefront of our minds, and what thoughts seem to fall away?

- How do we feel in our bodies when we can breathe more fully?

As we step back from the immediacy of our circumstances for a moment, let us welcome this rare opportunity for quiet. Let us consider what we can cultivate up here that will be valuable when we return down there. Perhaps it looks something like renewed tenderness, appreciation, and purpose.

Adopt a lens of grace

When I observe the lawn below, some students wander peacefully while others shuffle quickly, their backpacks bouncing up and down as they dart to their next commitment. As I notice how small they look, I can't help but consider my own smallness. I think about the pressure I put on myself to succeed, the heavy emotions I carry from imperfect relationships, and the disappointments that are an inevitable part of this life of longing and loss. No wonder this all feels so heavy—I am trying to carry it around in a backpack that is already loaded with textbooks and essays and a laptop. So, how can I lighten this load?

I wonder if a vital decision we must make is to let ourselves be imperfect. Maybe looking at the people below moving through their days with a blend of courage and fear reminds us that we are all in need of grace. A friend recently reminded me that when we take up the practice of extending ourselves grace, we are more likely to extend grace to others as well. I tucked her words away as a valuable token of wisdom. The way we treat ourselves and the way we treat those around us matters; they are inextricably linked.

Let us welcome the chance to consider where we see a reflection of ourselves in the people below. Do we see ourselves in the girl racing across campus with her eyes glued to her flashcards, nearly tripping over herself on the way to an exam? Or do we recognize the look of sadness in that boy's eyes as he mopes around with his headphones in, wanting to block the world out for a while? Perhaps we can grow in compassion for ourselves and others as we look at our campus from a unique angle.

Look for beauty

I still remember the first time I walked out of LensCrafters wearing a pair of glasses. I was in seventh grade, and my new glasses had a brown tortoiseshell pattern. Suddenly, the blurry parking lot came to life. Every detail on the green leaves and every letter on the license plates was crystal clear.

If you had asked me to describe the intricacy of those leaves or read a street sign from far away before I got my glasses, I would not have been able to. Even with all the effort I could muster, without those lenses, it would not have been plausible.

Part of gaining perspective is not only learning how to see our problems in a new light but also looking for the beauty around us that these problems initially obfuscate. And yet, it is often not as simple as making a choice. When we feel our circumstances enclosing us, our capacity to appreciate our blessings diminishes. Instead of being hard on ourselves for struggling to notice the goodness in our lives, we need to take action to refine our sight.

As you stand up here, take a moment to reflect on the past week of your life. If it was a hard week, you may only recall unpleasant moments at first: that pain in your shoulders from bending over your textbooks for hours, the anger you felt at a friend who lied to you, the anxiety about your exam. But as you continue to reflect from a distance, you may be surprised by what comes to mind: the friend who sent you an encouraging text before an exam, your roommate's thoughtful gesture, the kind dining worker who asked you how your day was going.

Maybe getting perspective is a little like putting on glasses. Taking a step back allows us to rekindle the hope we lost when our circumstances overwhelmed us. This hope not only reminds us that life can get better but that there may be good available to us right now. When we expand our vantage point, we create space to remember this good. And if we can practice appreciating beauty up here, it may be easier to do when we come down.

Consider your story: "the 30,000-foot view"

This retreat from the noise below also offers us space to reflect on the larger story of our lives and the values we want to live out.

I was listening to a podcast discussion with a group of Pixar screenwriters when my ears perked up at the mention of a concept called the "30,000-foot view." The writers use this term to describe the process of zooming out from a specific scene and considering its place in the overall story. In storytelling, it is just as important to articulate a character's transformation journey over time as it is to write a powerful scene.[3]

As we sit here together, 30,000 metaphorical feet above our own stories, let us discover hope as we realize that this day—with all its triumphs and losses—falls into a greater story we are telling with our lives. Here, we have the chance to ask ourselves questions like:

- When all the noise of this day fades away, what is the song I want to hear pulling me forward? Is it one of hope? Of peace? Perhaps it is one of continuing bravely even when I can't see what's ahead?

- Who do I want to be? How do I want to treat myself and the people around me when things don't go my way?

- What contributes to my sense of hope? Is it a dream career I am working toward that motivates me on hard study nights, the love of friends who laugh with me after a long day, or my faith in a God who carries me through the darkest valleys? (Reminder: it can be little things and big things.)

As I gaze over my campus, I remember the way it looked when I was a prospective student, asking myself whether I could call this place home. I felt a sense of peace and expectation. A feeling of safety in the familiar and wonder for the novel all at once. I remember why I came here: to fall in love with this place, these people, and life itself. To learn and grow and change, even if it was scary and uncomfortable at times. To discover meaning, hope, and love, even if I could not articulate it when this began. To live. I came here to live.

Considering the larger themes in our lives is not an act of ignorance but of intention. Stepping back from our stressors for a little while does not mean that we believe they will magically disappear. But it enables us to consider how our response to these stressors might align with our deepest values, instead of acting impulsively. And seeing this moment in time as part of a larger story reminds us that while the pain may seem all-encompassing, it will not last forever. One day, we will see these circumstances in a new light.

Return to the ground

Unfortunately, we can't stay up here forever. I know this can be hard to accept. It is funny that we were resistant to stepping away at first. We wondered if the world would keep spinning without us for a little while. And yet, now that we are here, where life seems simpler, we are reluctant to return.

When I was growing up, my mom would often close out our time on vacation by saying, "All right, back to reality." Her words always frustrated me. I wanted to scream, "This is reality! This is the real world. Why do we have to act like a return home means a 180-degree turn away from the peace we have found here?"

Now that I am older, I understand her dismay at returning to our normal routine. And yet, I still don't think that we have to create such a large distinction between these moments of retreat and the reality of our day-to-day lives. We can steadily transition back to our specific circumstances without losing the peace that we found here. We must return to the problems that wait for us below. But we are not without perspective, and we are not without hope.

Now it is your turn

Think of the places on your campus that give you that feeling of peace. Or, if you are preparing to go to college, think of the kinds of places where you want to find comfort. The places that hold you as you sit or stand in silence. The places where can you step away, even just for a few minutes, and remind yourself that you are more than the stress you carry and the mistakes you have made. Maybe it is a room that overlooks the green or a bench at the top of the hill. Maybe it is inside a church illuminated by candlelight or a campus labyrinth where you can wander.

Find a location where you can remember why you came here in the first place. Search for a haven where you can leave the noise of your worries below because they can't reach you here. For a little while, let the bigness of the world comfort you rather than overwhelm you. Let it remind you what a gift it is to be small—to be finite—for when we take our eyes off ourselves for a moment, we get to bask in the beauty of being part of something much greater. Part of a community of justice-seekers and artists and inventors and those who peek into the meaning of it all for the rest of us. Part of the rhythms of this place. Where the sun rises and sets. Where people chatter all day and then retreat to the library to listen to the sound that books make in our silence. Where we love and we lose, and we get back up the next day because our hope is strong enough to wake us from our slumber.

As you spend time here, remember the practices we learned together—to change your vantage point, adopt a lens of grace, look for beauty, and consider your story from a "30,000-foot view." And then, when you are ready, return to the ground with a new perspective.

Perspective gives us a reason to shout—a reason to say what matters most. To ourselves. And maybe even to the people below, who wait with giddy smiles as rain clouds their vision. But it doesn't really matter. Because you can see them. And they can hear you. And somehow none of us are alone here anymore.

CHAPTER 13

A GRADUATION TO FORGET

On Coping With Fear

Dear resident,

A long line was already forming outside the chapel as we pulled up to my older brother Steven's college graduation ceremony. The next few moments transpired so quickly that I can't recall which order the words were spoken in, but I still remember the way they sounded. Dad's words of caution: "Diana, don't get out of the car yet." And Mom's scream: "Ahhh, get off me! You're on top of me with the car." And then the panic. It hit me with such force that I suddenly felt helpless. I wanted to disappear—to be anywhere but there.

But I couldn't slip away. I was stuck there. Stuck in the flowery patterned, navy dress that I had worn proudly to an Easter service a few weeks earlier. Stuck in the space between the image I had already created in my mind of

Mom's crushed body and the reality I would find if I was brave enough to face the unknown. Two different images, connected by one thread of fear.

After Dad finally moved the car forward and put it in a parked position, I took a deep breath, prayed a desperate prayer, and ran around the back of the car.

I let out a sigh of relief. She was okay.

But that didn't mean she wasn't hurt. Her foot had gotten caught under the tire, and we would later learn that several of her foot bones were broken.

The sound of someone saying a paramedic was coming brought me back to myself. *There's already an ambulance nearby. They will be here soon.*

While we waited, we put her in the back of the car. I ran around the other side and scooted into the seat, wrapping my arms around her. She has a very high pain tolerance, but I could tell she was struggling to cope. She leaned against me as my chest moved quickly in and out. Mother and daughter wrapped in love. Holding her as she once held me.

With fear and courage,
Elizabeth

What now?

It seems unfair that so many good moments in our lives can be lost to the folds of time, yet the ones we wish to forget play over and over in our minds. Somehow, the same sickness fills us with each replay as if we were experiencing it for the first time. As I think back to that day, it wasn't the sight of my mom on the ground that scared me the most. It was the dreadful scream that interrupted this ordinary car ride. It was those few seconds when the image I created in my mind was far worse than what I would end up finding. I wanted to forget that moment had ever happened. But I couldn't.

As you think back on memories from your past, which moments would you give anything to forget?

I know that these moments are terrifying, and I know they can stay with us for months or even years. We carry them around in our bodies and see how the fear that was birthed in an instant seeps out in subtle ways later—in our overprotection of loved ones, our tight chest when we wake up in the morning, our anticipation of bad news throughout the day, and our spiraling thoughts as we fall asleep at night.

These moments don't have to appear extreme externally to profoundly impact us internally. What leaves an indelible mark on our lives may not do the same for someone else. Some experiences may feel more dramatic than others, but I think we will recognize them by the unwanted influence they still have on our lives. The emotions tied to these moments can act as a rope, pulling us back in time toward the epicenter of the event and tethering us to it, restraining us from moving forward.

If you are like me, these moments spark a flood of questions: *What do I do with this? How can I possibly see the world through a lens of hope when I know that life can hold so much pain and fear? Will I ever be able to move lightly through the world again?*

I don't pretend to have the perfect answers to these hard questions.

At least no answers that will satisfy me enough to stop asking them. And I don't pretend to be an expert in working through the distressing events that leave me spiraling in the days and months to follow. But I can share what this healing process has looked like for me, not just in the wake of the accident but also after other moments that filled me with fear. I can share the searches for hope I've undertaken in those times when I was reminded of how heartbreaking life can be. Hope that I found in small things, surprising things. **While we might not be able to change painful memories from our past, we can discover a little bit of hope in the present as we come to see compassion, beauty, and love as great life rafts when we feel like we are drowning in fear.**

It is okay to cry

In one sense, the busyness of that day kept me pretty well distracted, which was probably for the best because I am prone to letting my thoughts spiral. And yet, I wonder if moving so fast through the graduation festivities prevented me from acknowledging just how distressing that moment was for me. If I could change one thing about that day—aside from the accident—it would have been this: I would have sought out a quiet, safe space to cry.

Instead, I sat through the graduation ceremony and forced myself to fixate on the sea of blue robes marching across the stage below, cheering loudly for Steven to fill in the silence of my mom and dad's absence. Following the ceremony, I participated in picture-taking, happy hour at a local residence, and dinner at a restaurant where we stayed late into the evening. The day felt like a whirlwind of activity that I was white-knuckling my way through. If I had just found a safe place to cry instead of distracting myself with activity, I think I could have returned to the festivities and been more emotionally present.

Do you remember when we were children and did this so well? Yet, somewhere along the way, we bought into the lie that burying our emotions was a sign of strength. If you are like me, you have been led to believe that after a challenging event has passed, the emotions that arose from it inevitably passed with it. But the truth is that most of us carry these feelings until we can find a way to release them.

In my experience, it is not enough just to reason my way out of distress. Reminding myself that the danger has passed is certainly a good place to start. *I am not in danger anymore. Mom is okay. I am okay.* It is helpful to ground ourselves after our feet have been kicked out from under us. But truths about the present moment do not change the reality of the past. *It was scary. Mom was hurt. And I was afraid.* These are facts that I wish I could change.

And it is okay to cry over them.

Though I didn't experience the catharsis I wish I would have on that day, there are other moments in my life when I did. One evening, about a year post grad, I found myself seated in front of a trusted friend expressing anger and sorrow that I had experienced so many painful days with a confusing health challenge. While I had voiced my frustration several times during that season, this time was different. I started to sob. My body shook as I let tears pour out of me. My voice cracked and strained as I tried to translate the torrent of emotions into coherent sentences. I am not sure how long it lasted, but I remember that when I was finished, my throat was sore, my nose was congested, and I was physically exhausted.

More than anything, though, I remember feeling so light. I remember feeling free. On the heels of a dramatic release of anger, fear, and regret, I could move forward and enjoy the strides toward health that I had made. Discovering hope did not look like ignoring the memories that made me question my relationship with hope in the first place. Instead, it looked more like creating space for hope to grow on top of the soil of dreams lost in that painful season of my life.

Think of a time when you released your emotions in a rather unfiltered, unglamorous way. How did it feel? Although you may have felt embarrassed at the time, did you experience relief when you finally let go of feelings that were welling up in you?

Recall the painful memory, or memories, you identified at the beginning of this chapter. Consider what it might look like to release the emotions you may still be carrying. You don't have to do this all at once. It may look more like many small moments of release. But don't underestimate the power of this release. And don't hold back tears that need to come out.

Find safe people and safe places

Do you want to know what I so often forget when I feel weighed down by the pain of the past or anxious about the future? I forget that I don't have to go through the pain alone. And I think that in itself is a miracle.

When we are processing an event from our past when our sense of safety was uprooted, one of the most helpful gifts we can give ourselves is the chance to do so with safe people in a safe environment. In her book *Try Softer*, psychologist Aundi Kolber shares, "One hallmark of both big T and little t trauma is that the memory of the event isn't normal. Instead of recalling something as though it happened in the past—as if we were looking at a photograph while talking about it—we experience it as though it were happening in the present."[1]

Kolber gives language to the experience that many of us have undergone as we relived painful memories with such visceral reactions.

Her explanation makes me realize just how essential it is that we feel safe when we recall these experiences, whether it is right after they occur or many months later.

Although we may have felt alone when we experienced the event in the past, we do not have to relive it alone. We do not have to work through the distressing thoughts, feelings, and physical responses that this recollection might bring up on our own. This work of processing painful memories should not be a solitary job. What relief we can find in that!

Now, I must admit something. When I hear the word *process*, I feel myself tensing up. I have been in communities where this word was thrown around a lot, and honestly, I sometimes wonder if it is overused. Images come to mind of a person "processing" their breakup with a dozen friends—reliving the anticipation, breaking point, and fallout over and over again as each person asks the same prying questions. This sounds exhausting. And I suspect it often satisfies other people's curiosity rather than helping the person who is sharing their story. But it should not be this way.

So, what does it look like to process a troubling memory healthily?

I will use the example of therapy because it has been transformative in my own life. But I am not claiming that therapy is the only way that we can safely process the past.

For many years, I avoided therapy because it sounded frightening and uncomfortable. The idea of picking apart my emotions and past hurts with a stranger filled me with trepidation. But when I finally decided to meet with a therapist over the summer after my sophomore year, I came to realize just how helpful it could be.

From the beginning, I was surprised by how safe I felt talking to a woman I had only just met. I could be honest there. I could be scared. I could revisit the past in a safe space with a safe person. And I could believe that healing was possible.

I learned that wise and trustworthy people can offer a perspective on our situation that we may be unable to see in the present moment. They may point out truths that we are struggling to believe because of what we've been through. And with gentle encouragement, they may propel us toward the hope of healing when we have been spinning in circles for so long that we can't see which direction it is in.

No matter how much I try to avoid facing this truth—life *is* unpredictable. Even if we proceed with great caution, accidents still happen. Grief meets us whether we are prepared for it or not. And sometimes, people hurt us in deeply unfair ways. There will be moments when we don't believe that real healing is possible after what we have gone through. But when I find myself struggling to see beyond the present pain and I am feeling too weak to give myself a pep talk, I remind myself of this simple truth: I am not alone on this healing journey. And suddenly, it feels a little less scary.

When I remember the shoulders that I have cried on, the ears that have listened with tenderly withheld judgment, and the hearts of the people who have loved me as I did the hard work of seeking hope in the middle of unwelcome circumstances, I feel a newfound strength and courage. I think of Anne Lamott's words, striking and soft all at once: "Love has bridged the high-rises of despair we were about to fall between. Love has been a penlight in the blackest, bleakest nights. Love has been a wild animal, a poultice, a dinghy, a coat. Love is why we have hope."[2]

It won't always feel the same

A friend shared a helpful metaphor with me for the long-term process of grieving, called "growing around grief." In a 1996 research article, counselor Dr. Lois Tonkin presented this alternate view of grief because she had learned from her clients that not everyone appeared to move through the stages of grief to the "resolution stage." For some individuals, the grief remained just as large, but they learned to grow around it, expanding their lives so that the way they carried it changed.[3]

I wonder if something similar happens to us as we begin the difficult but worthwhile work of processing a painful moment from our past so we can move toward healing. Recalling distressing memories can feel a lot like grief. We grieve everything we lost when we learned that life is far messier than we hoped it would be. So maybe we too can learn to grow around our grief.

There is something comforting about the possibility of change, isn't there? Instead of wishing away our memories of the past, it might feel less intimidating to simply ask ourselves what it might look like to develop an evolving relationship with them. Just as we change with the passing of seasons and years, the hurts we carry can evolve too. Like scars from a physical injury, emotional wounds can fade as well.

I believe that we can find hope by recalling our own past experiences of healing. Think of moments from your past when the future felt so uncertain. When you could not see beyond the wall in front of you because the blocks you stood on kept toppling over. As you reflect on those memories many months or years later, is it true that you made it to the other side of that wall? Is it possible that what sparked this fear in you no longer holds the same grip as it once did? Isn't it amazing how your perception of those moments has changed, even when you believed it was impossible? Sometimes, we heal surprisingly fast. Other times, healing moves so slowly that we can hardly believe it is happening. But whether your healing came quickly or slowly, don't discount your own testimonies as proof that you can find freedom from the burden of residual fear.

The panic you feel when you think about that moment won't stay the same forever. You may never be able to return to the memory with detached emotion, but that doesn't make you weak. You are human and it was really scary. And over time, with healing and love, the way you carry that experience can change.

We can still believe in goodness

Perhaps my greatest fear when I face the unforgiving brunt of pain—whether I am witnessing a troubling scene, walking beside a loved one who faces a tragedy, or enduring a particularly unpleasant bout of sickness—is that my capacity to delight in my life will be dampened. I fear that these moments will irrevocably change me and the way I see the world. I guess to an extent that every big event in our lives does, whether it is a commencement ceremony that marks our passing from one stage into another or the incident that occurred outside the chapel.

When I find myself particularly saddened by this thought—that these precious human gifts of amazement and wonder and abounding gratitude are no longer within my reach—I remind myself of these beautiful and remarkably honest words from Kate Bowler: "I can't reconcile the way that the world is jolted by events that are wonderful and terrible, the gorgeous and the tragic. Except that I am beginning to believe that these opposites do not cancel each other out ... I think the same thoughts again and again. Life is so beautiful. Life is so hard."[4]

During a particularly painful season of my life, I wrote these words over and over again. "Life is so beautiful. Life is so hard." I drew them in fancy letters decorated with flowers and placed them in my kitchen and on my bedroom wall. I let them wash over me, permitting me to feel grateful and angry all at once; to welcome in awe and heartbreak, healing laughter and weary tears.

May these words be your anthem when you do not want to choose between feigning gratitude and letting suffering overwhelm you. May you give yourself the grace to feel all of it—the ache of being human and the marvel of being alive.

What would it look like for you to revisit a painful memory in a safe space so you can thoughtfully look for compassion, beauty, and love?

When I remember my brother's graduation day, I can certainly see small glimmers of light that soften the blow of harsher moments. I recall the compassion that Steven's friend's mom showed me when she invited me to sit with her family during the ceremony. I remember the beautiful friendship between Steven and his closest friends—who made each other laugh like nothing I had witnessed before. And I saw love in the tender way that Steven carried Mom to the car as rain poured from the sky.

I do not mean to insinuate that this intentional recollection will take the pain away or make up for the unfairness stitched into the fabric of our lives. But if the song "life is so hard" is so loud that it muffles "life is so beautiful," then this exercise might be helpful. Ask yourself what you often miss when you return to that moment. Perhaps the moment itself was terrible, but in the days that followed, you witnessed the kindness of friends and the generosity of strangers. Maybe you even surprised yourself by displaying a beautiful form of courage. This is how you will begin to discover hope—by deliberately searching for what remains in the wake of loss.

It might not be particularly loud, but the hope we uncover will be enough to draw us forward. It will be enough to keep us awake to the world around us. Awake to the love that circles us, pulling us out of ourselves when all we want to do is collapse inward. A love that expands to fill our hearts so the fear that threatens to engulf us has no room to grow.

CHAPTER 14

13.1 MILES

On Moving Forward

Dear resident,

Rain pummeled the runners as we shouted our support from the sidelines. Our voices rang out through the frigid April air, caught by racers for a moment before they flashed out of our field of vision. When our throats hurt from cheering and our fingers ached from the cold, all we had to do was look at the determination on their faces, and a newfound motivation invigorated us to continue standing in the rain for hours, playing our small role in this historic event.

I watched my first Boston Marathon in a massive rainstorm, standing beside the 21-mile marker sign on the edge of BC's campus at the bottom of "Heartbreak Hill." The extreme weather only heightened the momentous feeling of that day. Witnessing thousands of people display extraordinary perseverance was inspiring, and I felt like I belonged to something special.

Four days later, I found myself several miles away from campus on an early evening run. I hadn't planned to run that far when I began. But inspired by the marathon racers, I challenged myself to run farther than I imagined I could. I didn't have a number in mind for a while, but I just kept putting one foot in front of the other. And then I started to set small goals: *just one more mile*. And as each mile passed, I found myself inching closer and closer to a number I had never accomplished before.

Okay, I am almost at 10. Let me just get to 10. And then, *well, I've come this far. I wonder if I can run a half-marathon.*

For the last few miles, my throat burned and my legs wobbled. I was already back near campus at this point, so I slowly weaved my way through the adjacent neighborhood, passing the same houses over and over again. I am sure that I looked ridiculous, moving more like a tortoise than a human. But I remembered my brother's words—you can run farther than you think if you just go slowly. And he was right. It wasn't about how fast I ran, how quickly I finished, or who I compared myself to. It was about moving forward. One small step at a time. One breath at a time.

When I looked down at my phone and finally read that glorious number on MapMyRun, 13.1 miles, I was filled with an indescribable feeling of triumph. I didn't care how long it had taken me. I didn't care that it was not an official race. I had surpassed my expectations by miles. By the grace of God, I had achieved my own "impossible" feat.

Onward,
Elizabeth

A better approach to overwhelm

Can you think of a time in your life when you were standing at the beginning of a long road and couldn't imagine how you would make it to the end? Many experiences from college come to mind when I ask myself this question. Maybe you are working toward a degree that feels impossible to attain. Or perhaps the job search process feels never-ending and fruitless. Have you or a loved one received a diagnosis that scares you? Whether we are working toward a challenging goal or moving through a season of uncertainty, it is normal for discomfort to arise when we realize how little we can control.

In response to this discomfort, I often try to predict the scenery I will pass, the pain I will feel, and the strength it will require of me. But most of the time, I am just blindly guessing. Furthermore, I imagine a series of challenges as if they are happening simultaneously. *If I can plan for these potential scenarios now, then I can cope with them better when they happen, right?* Except all this "strategy" does is leave me feeling overwhelmed.

When we face life events that threaten our capacity for hope—such as an illness, an injury, a stressful academic load, heartbreak, or grief—we need an effective approach to move toward healing. Trying to meticulously plan when we don't know what the road will look like or how long it will take to travel not only is futile but can also be counterproductive. If the path in front of us looks daunting and overwhelming, we may start to lose hope.

So instead, I invite you to begin right where you are. At this moment, on this day, what will it take to just start walking? I am not asking you to take big steps, only to keep moving. **When we feel overwhelmed by the road in front of us, the best course of action is to move forward one step and one breath at a time.** As we do, we can wisely discern how to devote our energy, time, and resources toward our goal. And we can look around for people to support us because the best races are never run alone.

You may recall that I asked you to step back from your immediate stressors and think about the wider scope of your life in Chapter 13. In this chapter, I am asking you to shrink your field of vision. I have found both strategies helpful, depending on the situation. When we are so focused on one specific stressor that we start to miss out on everything else in our life, then gaining a wider perspective is vital. Conversely, when we are in a season that feels overwhelming and our minds start spinning with all the demands that life is throwing at us, we need to narrow our focus. In these times, the small-step approach can be remarkably powerful. There is freedom in focusing on the here and now. There is wisdom in dividing a long road into very small steps. And maybe we will see that as our ability to focus on the present improves, our capacity to hope for a brighter future grows with it.

Bite-sized pieces

In an article titled "The 15-Minute Rule," author Hannah Brencher shares her approach to making progress on larger goals. She simply focuses on taking action for 15 minutes at a time. She explains, "With just 15 minutes, I make progress in a direction that matters to me. I change the landscape around me and get closer to the goals that really matter to me. It's really all about looking for that tiny thread within a larger task and beginning to pull."[1]

What I love about Brencher's approach is that she is less focused on perfectly performing her tasks and more on making progress. Because she gives herself such a manageable goal, she is less likely to procrastinate or become overwhelmed in the process. And the closer she moves toward her goal, even in small increments, the more confident she is that she can actually reach it.

When it comes to getting through stressful days in college, this is a helpful strategy to adopt. If you are anxious about a big essay, you could spend 15 minutes mind-mapping the main points you want to make. If you are recovering from an injury, you could spend 15 minutes stretching or doing physical therapy exercises. If you have to clean your messy room, you could begin by organizing your desk for 15 minutes.

If you have ever prepared a meal for a young child, you know that before you serve it, you have to cut it up into bite-sized pieces so they don't choke. It is difficult for children to understand the portion size they can handle. But if we're being honest with ourselves, we often make poor decisions about our own metaphorical portion sizes. Sometimes, we underestimate our ability to eat anything (like trying to avoid a doctor's appointment because we're scared of getting our blood drawn) and other times, we take bites that are too big (like trying to tackle a seven-page paper in one night). The key is to get the right portion size so that we can move steadily toward our goal.

Here are a few examples:

- If you are coping with heartbreak, instead of discussing it with everyone in your life, it may be easier to find a few trusted people and schedule time to process it with them. This will give you peace of mind knowing you have a dedicated period to process your pain, freeing you up to focus on other responsibilities for the remainder of your time.

- If you are sick, instead of catastrophizing about how you will feel tomorrow or next week, focus on doing whatever you can to take care of your body today. Give yourself simple tasks like drinking water with electrolytes, scheduling a doctor's appointment, taking your medicine, or asking a friend to bring you food from the dining hall.

- If you are having a panic attack, focus on counting out your breaths. *Breathe in for four seconds, hold for four seconds, breathe out for four seconds, hold for four seconds. And repeat.* This is called box breathing. Don't focus on anything else; just count and breathe.

More than a finish line

During my junior year, I attended a campus ministry retreat called "The Art and Soul Retreat." It was a wonderful opportunity to take a break from my responsibilities on campus and find nourishment for my soul. While there were several solitary opportunities to create art that weekend, my favorite pastime was working on a communal art piece: the sand mandala.

Originally created by Tibetan Buddhists, a sand mandala is an art form that incorporates colorful grains of sand to produce a large intricate design, typically in the shape of a circle.[2] At the beginning of the retreat, one of our leaders sketched a design on a large round sheet of paper, and it was our job to fill it in with sand. To apply the sand, I folded a piece of paper in the shape of a funnel and poured my chosen color into the large end. Then, I held the small end over a portion of the drawing and moved my hand slowly as small grains escaped through the tiny opening at the bottom.

That weekend, I loved bending over the table with my hands gently clasping the funnel. I lost myself in the wonder of watching tiny grains join to create a beautiful, cohesive picture. I learned not to rush the process; it was not about finishing quickly but finding joy in filling empty spaces with color. I learned patience and discipline, how to follow a plan, and how to creatively pivot when I ran outside the lines. I enjoyed creating art alongside others. And I found peace as I concentrated on one small task while the rest of the world fell away.

On the last morning of the retreat, we finally finished the mandala. After spending a few minutes admiring our work of art, it was time to wipe it away. That sounds crazy, right? Except that is the very point of a mandala. Each time someone makes a mandala, they do so knowing it will not be preserved. The point is not to create something that will last but to enjoy the creation process itself. Although we cannot keep the final product, we can walk away from this experience as changed people. And that matters.

The lesson I learned from making a mandala reminds me of a phrase that my leadership council used when we were choosing our successors. As a council, we underwent a two-day-long deliberation process that lasted several hours with thoughtful discussion about each candidate. Before we began, our leaders told us, "The process is the product." It wasn't until the end of the weekend that I understood the meaning of this phrase. We had to learn to trust the process—to believe that the product was not its own entity but rather a direct reflection of everything that came before it. In this case, the process was made up of hundreds of comments, questions, and productive debates. Put simply, the product would not exist without the process.

Sometimes, we get so caught up in our end goal—in achieving one particular definition of healing—that we lose sight of the bigger picture. We forget to ask ourselves who we are becoming on this hard but worthwhile journey. What if hope is not just something that carries us through hard days until we finally reach our goal but also something we discover along the way? What if the very process of learning to be people who hope on the ascent up the mountain is just as significant as reaching the mountaintop?

Who are you becoming as you overcome challenges, whether you are trying to heal from a hard season in your past or pursuing a goal in your future? If you are rebuilding your relationship with food after a sickness, each time you eat something that once scared you, you are teaching your body to trust itself again. If you are training for a marathon, each time you wake up early and jump out of bed, you are practicing discipline. If you are working on a group project, the way you support your group members who are struggling matters even more than the final grade you receive. And as I have been writing this book, I know that the thrill of watching my ideas come to life is its own sort of magic, something that won't be affected by the experience of holding the final product in my hand.

A finish line can give us the motivation to move forward and a direction to move toward. But in the end, what matters so much more is the people we become as we courageously step forward into the unknown.

Acknowledging victories

The sentiment of leaning into the process is nice, right? But what happens when we start to lose motivation on this long journey? When we are not enjoying the process itself or are struggling to identify concrete rewards in this painful period, maybe what we need is the chance to celebrate a victory. Even if it is not *the* victory, small victories along the way are still worth acknowledging.

When I was struggling with agoraphobia caused by the period of illness I experienced toward the end of college, I wanted to return to who I was before fear crept in and added a heaviness to every area of my life. I wanted the fear to dissipate quickly, but my body had developed a conditioned response that led to symptoms of panic arising when I left my house, and it took a lot of work to decondition it. So, with my therapist, I identified small goals that I could accomplish as I worked toward bigger ones. At first, my goal was just to leave the house once a week.

On a piece of paper lined with colorful polka dots, I wrote "Victories" at the top. And beneath it, I recorded the times I left my house, especially when I was most afraid of doing so. Here are a few examples of what I wrote: *Driving to the airport to pick up my mom, playing tennis with my brother, watching a movie at the theater, and going to dinner with friends.* If you had asked me four years ago whether I counted these as "victories," I would have been confused. Because four years ago, I was traveling throughout Europe on my own, unaware of the impending fear that would swallow me up just months later.

Our victories will look different depending on the season of life we are in. It can feel silly to call something a victory that a few years before, we didn't have to think twice about. But I encourage you to let go of self-judgment and shame. Don't let others tell you what "should" be difficult and what "should" be classified as a victory. And don't let that voice in your head minimize your pain or the courage that it takes to push through.

It is so easy to discount the progress we are making, especially when real-life healing is a lot messier than it appears in movie montages. Growth is not a linear process, nor is it something that can be easily defined by onlookers. But we can identify what felt impossible when we started this race, even if it appears small to others. We know the significance of battles that require us to ask ourselves where we find our hope. And if something took courage and grit, then it is worth celebrating.

What is the power of acknowledging these victories? Well, when we take the time to see how far we have come from where we began, we can discover a newfound motivation for the road ahead. The acknowledgment of one victory gives us a boost forward—a tangible reminder that the next victory is within reach, even if it feels hard to attain. Little wins are worth rejoicing over. Even if nobody else sees them, we know they matter. And in a world that lauds big displays of success, I want to be someone who notices the smallest signs of growth. Because growth is growth, no matter how small. And when you think about it, it is pretty miraculous.

Growth like a plant

On my 23rd birthday, my friend Sara dropped off a pot filled with a bed of dirt and a few small clippings from her pothos plant. I was so excited to receive this gift because I had never owned a plant. And for the same reason, I was also a bit intimidated. The instructions she left were simple: *Just water when the soil is dry, and it will let you know when it is thirsty. It likes direct sunlight, and lots of it.* Despite these simple instructions, I honestly had little faith in my ability to keep this plant alive, let alone nurture it into a flourishing state. But I knew I had to try.

Every week, I did as she said, pouring a small amount of water into the pot and watching as the soil slowly drank it up. At first, I didn't notice much of a change, but I stuck with it. There was something therapeutic about caring for that plant. It didn't ask too much of me, just a weekly intention to water it and the discipline to follow through.

If you have ever cared for a plant, you will know that growth does not happen overnight. If we see it every day, we are too close to it to notice significant changes. This can make it difficult to believe that the work we are putting in matters. But it does, and over time, I noticed small changes. Little by little, the plant began to grow. When I compare my first photo of the plant and a photo of it on my 24th birthday, the growth is obvious. A year later, the plant is blooming with life. Its vines stretch with strength and its green leaves shine with vitality.

The growth process is similar for us humans. It is an amazing feeling to look at ourselves in the mirror, see how far we have come, and recall countless acts of courage that led us here. We can remember moments when we fell, ready to give up, only to get up again with newfound hope, determined to try again. Growth does not just happen; it requires time, care, and patience. And when we look back on how far we have come, we will see that we did not hope in vain.

Moving forward

I know the temptation to stay stuck in whatever hole life has knocked us down into. Whether it is a pit of depression, a spiral of anxiety, a quicksand of grief, or some other abyss of hopelessness, it feels impossible to find a way out. It is not that we want to stay stuck. In fact, we were made to be resilient, to survive, and to courageously overcome the challenges we face. But sometimes, we truly doubt that there is an escape. And the path toward healing feels even scarier than remaining in our *stuckness*.

Friend, I have been there. Trust me, I have been there. I know what it is like to walk the same lonely path day after day, wondering what happened to the life I once knew. I know what it is like to name my losses and imagine that is all they will ever be. I have known hopelessness and regret. And I have wondered why I should bother to keep believing that life can get better.

If you are in this place today, I don't want to give you a motivational speech to race ahead and conquer your fears all at once. If this is in your nature, then great; go for it. But for most of us, this approach just isn't realistic. We understand that growth does not have to look one way. And we know deep down that transformative healing takes time.

So instead, I invite you to adopt a lighter approach. Rather than focusing on the finish line, try to break your journey into "bite-sized pieces," embrace the process of healing, acknowledge small victories along the way, and look back at how far you have come with awe. Who you grow into as you climb out of that hole, one act of courage at a time, will amaze you.

Whenever you are tempted to abandon this strategy out of impatience or doubt, take a deep breath. Look for one beautiful thing around you, savor it, and then keep moving forward. Remember, the goal is not perfection but moving toward healing, however long it takes. Because, in John Green's words, "the light-soaked days are coming."[3] How beautiful these days will be. And I want us both to be here for them.

Applying the small-step approach

Before moving on to Part 3, take a moment to reflect on the lessons we have learned together about discovering hope in hard times.

I pray that the stories you have read will encourage you on your own journey through darkness and light. But I know that when we feel overwhelmed, it can be difficult to remember all the advice we have received. So, instead of trying to remember everything from these chapters, maybe you could begin by taking just one action step for each chapter.

Here are some examples of how you can apply this small-step mindset to the topics we journeyed through in Part 2:

- When you are grieving, find one way to honor the person you have lost.

- When you are struggling with your mental health, reach out to one trusted friend who you can confide in.

- When you are tired from carrying other people's burdens, make a list of your cares in your circle of influence and your circle of concern.

- When you feel engulfed by stress, find a quiet space on campus to retreat to for a while and gain perspective.

- When you are trying to heal from a painful experience, write a list of beliefs this event sparked in you and share it with a trusted friend or mentor. Ask this person to help you discern which beliefs are true and helpful, and which will no longer serve you.

I know the road is long, but we can walk it at our own pace. I know it feels lonely, but we do not have to do it alone. And I know the dense trees can block out the light overhead. But keep moving.

Just keep moving. I see a clearing up ahead. Can you see it too? The sun is pouring down, waiting to cover us with light. And I know we will get there, one brave step at a time.

PART 3

DISCOVER LOVE

LET IT BE LOVE

I remember sitting with new friends on a retreat as we shared breakfast over a long wooden table. We were making small talk when someone asked, "What gets you out of bed in the morning?" One of the leaders, an upperclassman in the School of Education, spoke about her students and the motivation they gave her. To be honest, I can't quite remember my answer. But I think it had something to do with love.

As I think back to the many mornings I woke up as a college student, I admit that love was not always the first thought on my mind. It was not always the reason I pulled off my blush comforter, swung my tired legs over my raised bed, and leaped onto my dorm room carpet. There were many reasons why I got out of bed: fear of failing a test, the desire to impress a guy in my class, a sense of responsibility to make the most of my education, or anxiety over a never-ending to-do list scrolling behind my eyes. There is nothing wrong with these motivations. But I think that sometimes, they can blind our view of what matters most. *How often do we forget that there is no greater experience than loving and being loved?*

Thankfully, as my day continued, there was often a moment when I awoke to this deeper desire for love. It was like a spark that recalibrated my system, a reminder of my purpose, a revelation of life's greatest gift. I realized that I didn't want to just ride the unpredictable roller coaster of my emotions and longings throughout the day. I wanted something steadier to cling to. I wanted love to lead me.

Maybe you have this same longing too. But like me, your mind and heart become distracted by other things. Sometimes, we look for love where other people tell us we will find it, only to be disappointed when we realize they were mistaken.

We fill up our social calendar for the weekend, but if the individuals we spend time with don't truly know us, then we start the week feeling empty. We hurry around from classes to meetings to grocery shopping, surrounded by people, but we don't take the time to look another person in the eyes. We share our opinion on online platforms, but more than anything, we long to be earnestly heard, even if by just one person. And we work hard to keep up the appearance that we "have it all together," but deep down, we just want someone to see us at our worst and love us anyway.

Friend, I know how hard it is to live in a culture that encourages us to garner admiration at the cost of authentic relationships. I understand the loneliness that arises from living in an increasingly disconnected world. And I empathize with the temptation to get distracted by the allures of popularity, productivity, and performance-based affection. In my own college journey, when I fell into these temptations, I was thankful to have people who pointed me back to where love can truly be found. You will read about some of these people in the pages to come and the moments they reminded me of what matters. A surprising encounter, a significant conversation, a realization that I belonged in a community, an ordinary day transformed by the extraordinary power of love. These moments are etched into my memory—reminders that we do not have to put on a show to be met with empathy and love.

After reading these stories, I pray that you will have a new pursuit when you wake up in the morning: to know and love others as you invite them in to know and love you. The kind of love that transforms us, heals us, and inspires us does not just happen. To discover it, we must approach people with humility, grace, and an awareness that our perspective on the world is not the only one that matters. We must show up as we are and give others permission to do the same.

Let us walk this beautiful road together. Let us watch with wonder as the landscape before us slowly changes. And just maybe, we will find that we walk away changed as well.

CHAPTER 15

21 QUESTIONS

On Shedding Assumptions Through Stories

Stories are a communal currency of humanity.

TAHIR SHAH[1]

Dear resident,

I remember the anxiety that arose within me when I heard the question, "What was the worst day of your life?"

My face heated up and my heartbeat quickened its pace as I squirmed on the hard surface of the wooden chair beneath me. I tossed the question in my head like a boomerang, wondering what memory it would retrieve and bring to the forefront of my mind. Peering out over the circle in front of me, I was thankful that I had chosen a seat midway through the lineup.

It was day two of RA training and we gathered in our dorm lounge, exhausted from hours of lectures. We were preparing to work together for the next year, supporting students, enforcing dorm rules to ensure resident safety, and hosting fun social events. Living and working together in close quarters necessitated trust. And we had little time to build it. Hence the exercise we were partaking in.

Our graduate assistant, a cheerful young woman with a warm demeanor, was leading the activity. She read from a list of questions that progressively deepened in intensity. We were going in order, each answering the questions without elaborating.

The question about the worst day of our lives was understandably one of the last ones. I listened intently as my peers responded one by one. Again and again, I was surprised by the answers they gave. Then it was my turn, and I surprised myself with what I chose to share, no doubt emboldened by the vulnerability of those who came before me.

Hearing people answer such a vulnerable question opened my eyes to the reality that we all have hard parts of our stories that have shaped us. It reminded me why it is so important to lead with compassion—because we will never fully understand the hidden wounds that people walk around with.

If you had asked me beforehand whether I had crafted stories in my head about the "types of people" who sat in that circle with me, I might not have admitted it. But as I listened to my new friends, I realized how much I had misjudged many of them based on our prior few interactions.

When we finished our meeting for the night, it felt like something had shifted within our group. There was a new-found tenderness present in our interactions. I spoke to my peers with greater empathy, sensitivity, and awe at all they had overcome. Maybe you think this is a manufactured result of a "sappy" exercise, but the activity actually opened the door for greater sincerity. With each answer, we peeled back the barriers we had put up and started to see each other more authentically.

With curiosity,
Elizabeth

Not without consequence

Although I wish I could say otherwise, I admit I still form assumptions about others in my mind. I will hear the way that a classmate speaks and assume they must not be thoughtful. Or I will notice the confidence in a colleague's voice and assume they are prideful. Assumptions might seem innocent. After all, we have to use a certain degree of wise judgment to navigate complex social settings. But here is the thing about assumptions: although we may keep them to ourselves, they are not without consequence. The way we feel about others and the beliefs we hold about their stories affect the way we talk to them, talk about them, and act toward them. The judgments we carry about strangers, acquaintances, and even dear friends direct our behavior in their presence.

As I reflect on the lessons that I learned in college about loving people more wholeheartedly, I think the first step is getting honest about the judgments we hold about others. Whether we want to form new connections, nurture existing relationships, or serve others with empathy, we must first learn to shed the assumptions that we have constructed. Then, we can replace our assumptions with a better understanding of the truth in the form of stories. **As we listen to each other's stories, we reignite our compassion, develop an appreciation for nuance, and grow a deeper love for each other.**

The prevalence of assumptions in the college environment

I think there are a few characteristics of college that make the tendency to form assumptions especially common. If we can learn how to identify this temptation now, then we will be more prepared to do so in the future. And the more cognizant we are of our assumptions, the more we can take intentional steps to overcome them.

One major reason why we form assumptions about our peers in college is because we are meeting so many people at once. Whether we are making plans for the weekend, choosing classmates for an important group project, or deciding which club to join, the personalities of the people we spend time with can greatly influence our experience. It is natural to want to discern who we should surround ourselves with. But when we are so focused on finding the "right people" to associate with, we forget to give our peers time to reveal themselves to us. College is a huge life transition, and many of us need time to acclimate to this new environment before we feel comfortable letting our guards down.

Additionally, in this social media-obsessed culture, most of our peers project the image they want us to see. So, while some assumptions that we make about our classmates paint them in a negative light, others may reflect exactly what they want us to think: that they are carefree, social, and successful. But these projections can be misleading. The stories we share on social media do not show the entire picture. Instead, they exacerbate the problem of oversimplifying our perceptions of others. When we believe they are doing better than they are, we limit our ability to connect with them over shared struggles.

Finally, the judgments we make about our peers can arise out of our personal insecurities. I confess that I find comfort in holding on to the assumptions that I make about others. It is as if appointing myself as "the judge" protects me from my own inadequacies. Like the more I can identify someone else's "flaws," the more my feelings of inferiority will fade. But deep down, I know how unhelpful and untrue this logic is.

When we believe the wrong story

If you know me, you know I love stories. Our stories shape who we are and who we want to become. They connect us to each other and give us language to describe how we got to where we are. But what happens when the stories we tell ourselves are not based on reality? We may not notice the effects of this decision at first, but over time, it will erode our ability to create meaningful friendships.

You probably know the adage, "Don't judge a book by its cover." Well, I experienced this lesson firsthand when I was living back at home after college. I was passing my neighbor's house when I saw a box of items in front of their house with a *FREE* sign. With curiosity, I peered into the box and smiled when I saw a coming-of-age memoir my friend had raved about. I excitedly grabbed the book, brought it home, and put it on my bookshelf. Before I even opened it, I began to imagine the story that would unfold.

A few days later, I pulled out the book and flipped to the front. Leafing through the first few pages, I was confused to find that the interior title did not match the cover. *Hmmm,* I thought. *Maybe the title is referring to the first section of the book. That must be what's going on.* I started reading the first page, hoping that it would all make sense. But the more I read, the more confused I was. The story sounded a lot more like a murder mystery than a coming-of-age memoir. Finally, I took the book jacket off to see the title inscribed on the hardcover. *The book had the wrong jacket!* No wonder I was so confused. And because of my confusion, I couldn't be fully attentive to the *actual story* unfolding before me.

It is funny how long it took me to realize that the cover was mismatched. But we do that in our relationships, don't we? When we fixate on a narrative that we've imagined about somebody else, it can take a while to return to reality. This dissonance is disorienting. Sometimes, we may be pleasantly surprised by the person we find behind the cover. Other times, we may be disappointed to discover that this person we envisioned in our head does not live up to our unrealistic expectations of them. Either way, we are doing a disservice to the real person before us, and we are robbing ourselves of the chance to know them as they *truly* are.

We build transformative friendships on the foundations of mutual trust and authenticity. So, if we don't prioritize *truly knowing* others, how can we expect to cultivate flourishing relationships? We shouldn't expect to be changed for the better by relationships that are built on false premises. Deep down, we all want to love the *real* people we meet, not the fictitious versions of them that we have imagined.

So, how do we do this? How do we rewrite the scripts we have internalized about our roommates and classmates and that barista we greet every morning for a polite exchange? How do we see them not just as a character in our story but as unique individuals worthy of having their own stories heard? How do we move from *hypothesizing* about them to actually *knowing* them?

Rewriting scripts and reigniting compassion

Like most transformations I've shared in these chapters, we may have an inkling of what's required of us, but the actual process of change requires courage and intentionality. To rewrite the scripts that we have created about the people we interact with, we need to put down our metaphorical pen, close our mouths, and listen. We need to invite them into the scriptwriting process. Who better to write their personal narrative than the person who lived it?

Now, what does this look like practically? I will share two experiences I had learning people's stories in college. Keep in mind that some communities you are involved in will have built-in opportunities for honest storytelling while other times, these conversations will arise more organically.

One-on-ones

At the beginning of my year as an RA, one of my responsibilities was to set up informal one-on-ones with my residents. For several weeks, I met with each resident to get to know them and hear how they were adjusting to life at college. It is amazing what you can learn about a person when you spend time alone together. My residents got honest about their family dynamics, experiences with loss, battles with depression, and excitement for this new stage of their life.

I was honored to be entrusted with both the precious and painful parts of people's stories. And I received their vulnerability as a gift—an offering of truth when it would have been easier to hide the less pleasant parts of their lives. I like to think they opened up to me because they trusted me. Perhaps they wanted the person who would supervise and support them to get a glimpse into the significant chapters in their stories. I imagine it made them feel safe knowing that if wounds from their past became tender once again, they would not have to explain themselves.

For many of us, college feels like a chance to start over. Maybe we want to reinvent ourselves and look into the future with expectation. But I think there is also a part of us that wants to share pieces of our story with someone who sincerely cares.

Telling stories from our past can be cathartic. Whether you are talking to a roommate, classmate, or new acquaintance, you can initiate this type of conversation. Of course, it is important to be respectful when someone makes it clear that they do not want to talk about their past. But I've found that many people appreciate the chance to respond to questions asked with genuine curiosity, especially in a culture where many conversations remain at surface level.

Here are some questions you can ask to begin learning about somebody's story:

- What is your relationship like with your family?

- What was your hometown like?

- What significant moment from your childhood shaped you most?

- Why did you choose to come to this college?

- Is there an experience from your past that sparked your interest in the major or career you are pursuing?

There is great value in knowing pieces of other people's stories. The stories that people tell us can act as a light, illuminating important truths as we continue our quest toward greater love. And it is this greater awareness of the roads others have walked that enables us to support them in specific ways.

Sharing personal stories in a communal setting

Halfway through my freshman year, I joined a leadership program comprised of about 25 students. Over the course of three semesters, we each had the opportunity to share our "story" with the group. At the end of each meeting, a few members would stand in front of the group and share experiences that had shaped them. We all interpreted the instructions in our own way. Some reflected on family relationships or personal development journeys, while others shared stories of loss or heartbreak. But every story revealed a new side of the person standing before us.

Through this experience, I learned that we can spend months working alongside people and still miss some of the most significant aspects of their stories. This isn't necessarily a bad thing. Instead, it is a reminder that our stories are complex and evolving. We cannot expect to learn someone's whole story in one setting. The more time we spend together, the more we can reveal these pieces to each other. And over time, we realize just how little we knew about our friends when we met them. With this realization, we can acknowledge the futility of assumptions altogether.

Listening and compassion

I now see that it was not enough to just be present for the revelations from my new and old friends. Instead, I had to truly listen to the words they shared and open my heart to the possibility of being changed by them. And little by little, the people standing before me were becoming more real to me than they had ever been. They had been hurt or loved or afraid or inspired. They had lived their whole lives up to this point, just as I had. They were just as human as I was. And as I listened, compassion rose inside me. In a culture that entices us to lead with judgment, compassion is a treasure and listening is the key.

One of my favorite reflections on the value of listening comes from a video called "Loving Speech and Deep Listening." In it, Zen Master Thich Nhat Hanh invites us to embrace listening as a form of compassion. He shares, "Listening to that person, I only have a purpose: give him a chance to suffer less."[2] How beautiful is that? So often, I listen to others because I want something from them. What if, instead, I could listen because I want to ease their burdens?

As we listen, we are changed. And like a spool of thread that slowly unwinds, we watch as our hearts soften and our grip on control loosens. Maybe the classmate we assume is hostile toward us is struggling to cope with addiction in their family—and their fear has caused them to close off from others. Maybe someone in our dorm has a preoccupation with cleanliness and it seems strange to us—but if we took the time to listen, they would tell us that this caution stemmed from facing a traumatic childhood illness.

Little by little, if we allow ourselves to *truly listen*—leaning all the way in—we will see how the roads we walked to get here have shaped each of us, for good and for bad. And as our understanding of somebody's real story grows, we will be able to respond with words or actions. There is something powerful about giving someone a verbal acknowledgment that the hard thing was really hard. And offering a hug; hugs help. When we are no longer clinging to our assumptions, our hands are free to offer the gift of compassion to somebody else—just as they give us the chance to rewrite our scripts and trade judgment for love.

An ode to nuance

In her popular TED Talk "The Danger of a Single Story," writer Chimamanda Ngozi Adichie reflects on her experience growing up in Nigeria and coming to college in America. Through several anecdotes, we learn that Adichie was on both the giving and receiving end of assumptions based on someone's nationality or socioeconomic status. With self-deprecating humor and profound insight, she illuminates our human propensity to presume that we know someone based on a singular piece of information. What is the danger of a single story? Well, Adichie explains, "The single story creates stereotypes. And the problem with stereotypes is not that they are untrue, but that they are incomplete. They make one story become the only story."[3]

Take a moment to think about the individuals you live with, work with, and study alongside. Is it possible that you have adopted a "single story" to understand any of these people? Do you assume that they will act based on the common stereotypes you have assigned to them? Or are you seeing them as unique individuals capable of surprising you and teaching you something amazing?

When we resist the temptation to typecast our peers, we acknowledge their inherent dignity. We would not want someone to read a few facts about us on a piece of paper and assume that they know us. Likewise, we must be careful to show others the same respect.

As I think about the importance of valuing each person's individual story, an interview with *New York Times* columnist David Brooks comes to mind. Reflecting on research he was doing for a book that involved reading psychology books and memoirs, Brooks said, "The psychology books are interesting. Memoirs blow you away. Each individual human life is way more interesting than a group of human lives.... Each individual life has those moments that defy anything you could put in a category."[4]

Did you get that? Isn't it freeing to realize that we can't put people into categories even if we tried? We are not problems to be perfectly understood or analyzed. We are living, breathing humans who long to love and be loved, and who mess up time and time again—in a million different ways.

There is something exciting about this invitation to approach the people we encounter with an open mind. It is as if our friends and classmates have layers beneath their exterior—and if we listen closely, we just might be privileged to behold the beauty in each layer. When we see and appreciate the unique thumbprint of each person we meet, I think we will fall more in love with life itself. What a marvel it is to live in a world where each person we encounter is miraculous in their own way.

Deeper love

In the end, the purpose of listening to other people's stories is not just to know their histories but to cultivate deeper love for them. When we can orient our hearts toward this end goal of love, then we can begin to ask ourselves what it will take to get there. For me, this has looked like stepping into the stories of those I encounter with a desire to love them in specific ways, rooted in everyday interactions.

There is something powerful that happens when we start to see the people in front of us in their unadorned states. Maybe our roommate breaks down about regrets from their past. Or we see the panic in our teammate's eyes that they try so hard to hide, and we remember how fragile they are—how fragile we all are. The more we lean into these moments, these planned or unplanned expressions of authenticity, the closer we are moving to love.

This is the kind of love that grows strongest in pure light. Just as a plant can distinguish between artificial light and sunlight, so too can our hearts detect falsehoods. It is as if we are sifting through filters, the kind we absorb and the kind we cast, until finally, we come across something rare and beautiful: a natural expression of humanity. A desperate cry, an unbridled laugh, a weakened spirit, a strengthened resolve. Humans living real human lives.

And so, we keep moving toward deeper love. Deeper love as we let go of our assumptions. Deeper love as we quiet our minds and lean in. Deeper love through the pages of our friends' stories that surprise us and scare us and amaze us and break our hearts. Deeper love as their stories become the ones we hold close to our hearts, treasuring them as if they were our own. Deeper love for the person sitting before us, showing us what true bravery looks like.

This is the power of stories. This is the power of listening. This is the power of love.

CHAPTER 16

FRIDAYS AT EAGLE'S

On Nurturing Deep Friendships

Dear resident,

If you were to ask me what I have learned about friendship, I would tell you about Fridays at Eagle's.

You could hear Eagle's Nest dining hall before you saw it—at least on a Friday afternoon. The steady hum of chattering voices grew louder and louder, greeting me as I walked up the stairs from the first floor and through the glass doors. Though it was crowded, I felt a sense of relief when I walked in on this particular day of the week. It was as if everyone had finally released the breath they were holding since Monday. I maneuvered around the long line of students waiting for an unreasonable amount of time to buy a salad (and the popcorn chicken topping that seemed to defeat the very purpose of buying a salad in the first place). And then I came to a stop in the middle of the dining hall.

Standing as firm as a lighthouse, I began to rotate my head slowly. My eyes were beams of light sifting through faces, scanning for a sight that always filled me with comfort—like the feeling you get when you find a place to call home in a big city that doesn't feel so lonely anymore.

Peering. Peering. Peering.

And then I saw them. And they saw me.

Will waved his long arm wrapped in military green at me. Nick sat across from him in a maroon BC athletic shirt with a wide grin on his face. I made a beeline for their table and greeted them with a smile. Laughing at the ridiculous amount of food that was on their plates, I pulled out the empty chair, a warm feeling flooding my body as I sat down, knowing this open seat belonged to me.

I met Will during orientation right before starting freshman year, and he introduced me to Nick about a week later. We met up one Friday afternoon in Eagle's Nest to get to know each other better. At the end of our lunch, Will's face brightened as he said, "We should do this every week!" And so we did.

These Friday lunches soon became a significant part of my week. Whatever unexpected turns my week took and however stressful my classes were, I knew there was Fridays at Eagle's to look forward to. I treasured this time with Will and Nick. There was a peace that formed in my body as we sat there unhurried, catching up on silly moments from the week and more serious struggles we were facing. I loved the way the dining hall slowly became less and less crowded as time passed, and the loud bustle of rush hour softened to a quieter hum as the dining staff locked up the serving stations for the day. But it was okay because we had countless conversation topics to sustain us.

Will and Nick introduced me to a sweeter way of building friendships. Perhaps without even being aware of what they were doing, they invited me to let go of my desire for an exciting social life and step into the beautiful process of nurturing deep friendships with people who truly care about me.

With gratitude,
Elizabeth

The appeal and limitations of an exciting social life

When we think about forming friendships in college, we often idealize the notion of maintaining an exciting social life. If you are like me, you fell into this mindset much earlier than college. In grade school, I often found myself seeking approval from my peers, changing my appearance or behaviors to fit in. When I started college, I carried this yearning with me. I aspired to be one of those people who always had weekend plans and waved to countless friends in the dining hall.

There is certainly nothing wrong with having an active social life. But if we are constantly seeking breadth instead of depth in our relationships, we will feel disconnected. When we value friendships based on their external appearance, we forget the importance of the *actual* experience they offer us, both in what we give and what we receive. The cost of this disconnect is that we may spend time with people, but not actually *know* each other. What a lonely feeling. Trust me, I have been there.

Furthermore, surface-level friendships won't sustain us when life gets hard. What we really need is friends who we can rely on—who will show up and listen to us when it counts. We need people who will be there when life falls apart. We need friends who we can call when we are overwhelmed and don't want to sit in the mess alone.

As you reflect on the stories I have shared so far, many of them involved people who showed up for me when I was not at my best. Through their loyalty, these friends have reminded me that we must invest in relationships, not just maintain them. **By nurturing deep friendships, we create the opportunity to know and love others while being known and loved. We do not find a sense of belonging in surface-level acquaintances but in our friendships with people who are with us through joyful and painful moments.**

Wading into deeper waters

Now, how do we actually do this? We all long to be known and loved, don't we? But sometimes, it feels safer on the surface. And sometimes, we genuinely don't know how to move into deeper waters. Maybe you are thinking, *Of course I want deeper friendships. But right now, at least I have people to hang out with, even if they don't know me well. That's better than being alone in my dorm on a Friday night.*

I had these same thoughts, and this experience is normal! Especially when you begin college, you meet so many new people and casually get to know each other. You don't have to start asking deep questions of your new friends right off the bat. And you don't need to feel pressured to discern whether your fellow residents or classmates will be your friends for life.

During this season of transition, just enjoy the process of becoming acquainted with an array of interesting people. Lean in when someone tells you about growing up in a town with one stoplight or shows off their impressive dance moves (I have a fond memory of the latter from Welcome Week). Ask the silly icebreaker questions that can actually prompt intriguing responses. And revel in the feeling of seeing familiar faces as you walk around a campus that is starting to feel a little more like home.

As time passes, it can be easy to continue spending time with the people we met at the beginning of college without asking ourselves if we can rely on them. We may settle for surface-level friendships because we don't know how to invite others into deeper experiences of connection. I know this seems like the safer option, but how many of love's marvels do we miss out on because we are too afraid to open our hearts to people who truly want to know us?

The nuts and bolts of nurturing deep friendships

Nurturing deep friendships is not a perfect science. Human beings are incredibly complex, and when you put a few of us together, our individual interactions and overarching dynamic will be completely original. How amazing is that?

But I have found there to be some special ingredients in friendships that allow us to go deep and stay connected even as we change and grow. These ingredients have been present not only in my friendship with Will and Nick, but also in other significant relationships

I cherish. So, while each one may look different, they all share versions of these "ingredients."

Vulnerability-based trust

At the beginning of the team effectiveness sessions that my dad leads with his corporate clients, he often guides them through an exercise called "personal histories." Participants answer three questions, the last of which is: "What was the most difficult or important challenge of [your] childhood[?]"[1] My dad says it never ceases to amaze him how powerful this exercise is and how brave people are in sharing really hard parts of their stories. As a result, many people who have been working together for years build a much deeper level of trust. This activity is based on Patrick Lencioni's principle of "vulnerability-based trust." Lencioni posits that vulnerability is key to building trust among teams. If a leader is not vulnerable and able to admit their weaknesses and mistakes, then team members won't feel comfortable to do the same.[2]

I have certainly found this to be true in my friendships. It is not surprising that the strength of my friendships grew in correlation with the peeling back of protective layers as we gave each other the gift of vulnerability. When I lived in Boston for the summer, I shared a room with my friend Anna. We began a regular practice of praying together in the evenings, opening up about our hopes, fears, and disappointments. Instead of sharing polished prayer requests, we got honest about how we were really feeling and the burdens we were carrying. This prayer time improved our shared trust, opening the door for deeper honesty in future conversations.

When we are honest about our weaknesses and fears, we give our friends permission to do the same. Trust is a core element of a healthy friendship. And it begins when we let each other in on the "real stuff," however uncomfortable it may feel at first.

Commitment

In college, it is easy to value commitments that have obvious consequences when we neglect them. If we miss a class, our grade might reflect our absence. If we forsake our responsibility to a club, the disappointment of our team members will be obvious. Sometimes, we prioritize formal commitments over our loyalty to our friends. But the truth is that we all miss out when we don't honor our friendships. People matter. Time after time, I needed to remind myself of this simple truth when my busy calendar tried to blind me from it. You won't regret making time for the significant relationships in your life. The rewards of honoring your loved ones with your presence and undivided attention are priceless.

Consistency

Though it only lasts for four years, it feels like we go through so many different stages during college. We try new clubs, change housing several times, begin a new set of classes every few months, and constantly meet new people. While these changes keep life interesting, I now recognize a hidden gift within my time with Will and Nick. Meeting with them on Fridays gave me the consistency that I craved. It kept me grounded when life spun around me.

When I am caring for my pothos plant, I don't pour a month's worth of water on it and expect it to be sustained for the weeks to come. Instead, I offer it nourishment in small amounts again and again. In friendship, too, we learn that consistency matters. And we are so fortunate when we get the chance to practice this, albeit imperfectly.

I am learning that friendships grow in subtle ways, often beneath the surface of the soil. Sometimes, our seemingly ordinary actions convey the things that we don't always say with our words. Showing up each week was our silent declaration that we mattered to each other.

Grace

And yet, life happens. If we make consistency the ultimate goal, we will be disappointed in ourselves or angry at each other for faltering. So, it must become a means, not an end. This is where grace comes in. Sometimes, we have to get creative about how we stay connected to our friends, adjusting to life's unexpected circumstances. With Will and Nick, some lunches were shorter than others. And sometimes, we missed lunch but opted to study together in the evening. With a group of my friends who live far away from each other after college, consistency simply looks like sending photo updates on Fridays. It doesn't require a superhuman effort to be consistent. But it reminds us over and over that we have people out there who love us. And I think that's pretty remarkable.

Reciprocity

You are worthy of having people love you all the way back. I know that terrible feeling of giving more than you receive, over and over again. You know when you play tug-of-war and the other team suddenly releases the rope because they don't care enough to try anymore? You fall flat on your butt—and it aches. Sometimes, it feels easier to settle. But just like in a romantic relationship, genuine friends are worth waiting for. They love you for you. They don't ask you to become someone you are not. And they stay in the game even when life gets hard. I sincerely want that for you.

The freedom of authenticity

Although the process of building deep friendships can be challenging at times, the rewards are so worth the effort. Among the many benefits of having genuine friendships is the freedom to show up as our authentic selves. This feels especially rare in a culture that often encourages us to conform to other people's standards to earn acceptance. Without facades, explanations, or rehearsed lines, we get to come just as we are.

My friend Becca knows how to make me feel loved, just as I am. Her love for me is not dependent on my ability to "perform" like a good friend. Whether I was hopped up on sugar bouncing through the dorm hallway as a freshman, sharing my dream of writing a book, or admitting my feelings of loneliness, she always found a way to express her appreciation for me. She reminds me that my silly mannerisms, wild dreams, and expressions of pain are all worthy of being met with love. Becca and I have certainly seen each other through some really hard days. The silly and the solemn, the celebrations and the disappointments, the joyful and the terrible. All of it comes with being human. And when we choose authenticity, we are free to journey through it together.

For Becca's 24th birthday, I made her a photo album of our friendship, showcasing memories from our college adventures (donning matching vintage BC dresses at a tailgate, dressing up in Christmas PJs with our friend Taylor, and baking chocolate chip cookies in my dorm kitchen). But it also holds memories from the last few years when we stayed connected across the country. These photos, although less Instagram-worthy, are my favorite. Screenshots of FaceTime calls pepper the last pages. We wear casual clothes and overly enthusiastic smiles. I often FaceTimed her from my bedroom, not worried about appearing presentable. And before hanging up, I always asked if we could take a screenshot. It wasn't about the photo itself but what it represented: that we were still there for each other, ready to listen and offer words of love, just as we were.

The marvel of belonging

Each one of us longs to belong. I think it is part of the human condition to want to be a part of something beautiful and long-lasting, and to know people would sense our absence if we weren't there. But unlike many of our desires in life, friendships are not something you chase. They are something you show up for again and again. And you can start right now.

A memory comes to mind as I think about how Will, Nick, and I fit together, although we were so different. I look back on that moment and know I belonged in that trio.

In the spring of my sophomore year, I attended the military ball with Will, who was in the Reserve Officers' Training Corps (ROTC). I wore high heels and a navy-blue dress, which I had to get hemmed because I am so short! We enjoyed delicious food and great company. When we returned to campus, we invited Nick over to Will's dorm and we all hung out till late.

At the end of the night, I decided to take the bus back to my dorm across campus. As I was leaving Will's dorm, he and Nick said they would accompany me to the bus stop. We walked together casually until we reached the top of the stairs—the last leg of our short walk. As I stood there in my high heels, the stairs felt more daunting than usual. I looked at these boys on either side of me and reached out my arms to wrap around theirs. They were strong and steady.

As we slowly descended the steps, I smiled and told myself to soak in this moment. I inked it into my memory as a reminder of what they had taught me and who we were to each other. Without saying a thing, they reminded me of what I already knew to be true: when I was unsteady, I could lean on them—and they would not let me fall.

CHAPTER 17

WALKING
WITH HELEN

On Beholding Strangers

Dear resident,

I was circling the reservoir on a late afternoon stroll one spring day of my sophomore year. After a stressful week, I sought sanctuary in the serenity of this familiar place. As I neared the end of the loop, I took a seat on an empty bench and peered out over the reservoir. There was something about the gentle ripples of water that always calmed my restless heart.

After a little while, I lifted my eyes to see a middle-aged woman walking past me. Though it was a fairly warm day, she wore a large black parka, and gloves covered both of her hands. We must have made eye contact because she said hello. I responded in kind, and she seemed pleasantly surprised.

"Most people don't say hi to each other anymore," she exclaimed. I agreed, and we discussed the power of this simple gesture. After exchanging a few polite words, I asked if she would share some of her story with me. She accepted my invitation, and we decided to walk around the reservoir as we talked.

I quickly realized that this was not an ordinary encounter with a stranger. This woman, who had introduced herself as Helen, was surprisingly honest. She was sharing her story with a young woman a third of her age, finding her eager and ready to listen. By revealing some significant setbacks that she had faced, she gave me space to acknowledge her pain and honor her bravery.

As I walked with Helen, I realized just how much I craved human connection. Not the kind we build over text or by exchanging rushed pleasantries in the dining hall. But the kind that requires us to look up from what we are doing and walk at someone else's pace for a while. I smiled as I remembered an unconventional assignment that my Organizational Behavior professor had given us earlier that week. The instructions were to behold another person for an hour and then reflect upon our experience. How fortunate I was to have such a rich encounter to write about.

As we said goodbye, we were no longer just looking at each other but joyfully beholding one another. I remember walking away from her with a profound lightness that I carried with me for the rest of the day.

Walking with Helen filled me with a renewed sense of possibility. Our exchange reminded me that each of us holds treasures, but they often remain hidden from the people we pass by. In his book *The Weight of Glory*, C. S. Lewis says, "There are no *ordinary* people. You have never talked to a mere mortal."[1] As I listened to Helen's story and gratefully received her advice, I became convinced of this truth, and I wondered what my life would be like if I started to see strangers the way I saw Helen.

In awe,
Elizabeth

Seeing people as art

What does it mean to behold another person? When I ponder this question, I recall a conversation that I had with my friend Josie about her Art History class. Josie considered the awe with which she observed the magnificent works of art that she was studying, and then she compared it to the way she viewed people. To her dismay, she realized that she often viewed art pieces with more reverence, even though she knew that people were infinitely more precious.

Josie told me she wanted to begin seeing the people she encountered with a greater sense of wonder. And I don't know about you, but I think that's a beautiful desire. *What if we could see people like beautiful works of art?*

I imagine if we started seeing every person through this lens, then our appreciation for them would grow. Instead of labeling the guy asking for donations as an annoyance to be avoided or the woman with the squeaky grocery cart wheel as a stranger blocking the aisle, they could be so much more than that.

It may feel easier to apply this mindset to your view of close friends and family—but what about someone you have just met? What about a stranger? In this day and age, it is easy to move through our days without really acknowledging the strangers who cross our paths. We get wrapped up in our own responsibilities and commitments, measuring a successful day by the number of tasks we accomplish, and we forget that productivity alone does not make a good life.

But when we take the time to behold the strangers we encounter, we experience the gift of connection—not because we have known them for long, but because we see their beautiful imperfect humanity and recognize our own in the process.

More than an interruption

A few years ago, my friend was describing her experience shopping in a grocery store when she was in a hurry. She said that she saw the individuals she passed as "blank faces" rather than real people. If we're being honest, we all can probably relate to that from time to time.

How often do we weave through the store, the dining hall, or the dorm hallway without making eye contact with the individuals we walk by? We look down at our phones. We use the self-check out line. We trade real connection and an acknowledgment of each other's humanity for convenience, speed, and comfort.

My hope is that through the remainder of this chapter, you will come to see strangers as more than interruptions, annoyances, or means to an end. This includes the guy who asks you for directions when you are late to class, the girl who is holding up the salad line with her complicated order, and the woman whose job it is to complete that order. We may see these people as mere inconveniences in our story. But there is a danger in assigning value to people based on how they affect our plans and wellbeing. In doing so, we start to believe that our story is the only one that matters—and we forget that each person we meet is living their own valuable story.

On his website The Dictionary of Obscure Sorrows, John Koenig created a term to describe this important realization. He called this word "sonder." Here is a condensed version of the definition: "The realization that each random passerby is living a life as vivid and complex as your own—populated with their own ambitions, friends, routines, worries and inherited craziness."[2]

We need people like Koenig to remind us that although we may feel like the center of *our own* world, we are not the center of *the* world. While many of the people we pass by might be minor characters in our story, they are just as worthy of love.

If we really want to trade our indifference toward a stranger for sincere interest, we can't just continue to observe them from afar. We must reach out and give them a chance to reveal their unique identity to us.

Start with a question

Maybe you are waiting in line to pick up textbooks in the bookstore basement. You know, the long line that snakes around the corner and never seems to move forward an inch, despite the mind power you are devoting toward manipulating it. You are surrounded by other students who are staring at their phone screens or the specks of dirt on the gray carpet. Nobody wants to be there—that much is clear. But you are not alone. You are literally one foot away from people on either side of you. So, who will it be? Pick a person, lean in, and ask a question.

You choose the guy with the baseball cap and sweatpants. *What classes are you taking? Where are you from? How's your day going?* Anything works as long as you are genuinely interested in his answer.

How will he respond? Only time will tell. Maybe he gives you a polite response but wants to be left alone. That's okay as we want to respect people's boundaries. Sometimes, we just have to endure the silence.

But maybe he will respond enthusiastically, pleasantly surprised that you engaged with him, and the conversation may continue to evolve. If so, ask him to share parts of his story with you, and do more listening than speaking. When you don't know what questions to ask, let the silence hold you together. Sharing silence with another human does not always mean that you are giving up on a conversation; it can also be an invitation to go deeper.

Instead of trying to assuage your own boredom, get excited about the chance to become acquainted with someone you didn't know before. If you think about it, that's pretty remarkable. If you go out of your way just a bit, you can end the day having spoken to someone who you didn't even know existed when you woke up. They have been walking around this great big world, living each day of their life just as you have, and today is the day you get to meet.

There is something powerful about appreciating somebody's existence, regardless of their relation to us. To be thankful not only for our ability to interact with them, but also that they are in this world at all. This is an important part of stepping outside our own little spheres. To love someone for who they are, not just for how they add to or detract from our lives. This is a step in the right direction. I know this in my heart.

Offering our attention

You know those people who can stare at a piece of art for what feels like an hour, appreciating every intricate detail of it and honoring the work that went into creating it? I imagine if the art could talk, it would say thank you. It would be grateful for the chance to be admired and intimately known. Now, as humans, how much more do we crave that?

When I think of the value of offering another person attention, I think of a Saturday evening I spent in an unassuming Starbucks near campus where I struck up a conversation with a middle-aged woman named Mary.

I was sitting on my little stool as she stood before me—my back to the bar and her back to the sky darkening through the storefront window. The day was coming to a close, but something beautiful was happening in this place: two strangers were opening their hearts to each other.

She spoke about her faith, which she was still exploring (aren't we all, though?). She reflected on some deep losses in her life, and my heart swelled with sadness for her. I imagined the loneliness that accompanied such loss and hoped that by listening, I could help her feel less alone for a little while. She spoke of washing her clothes at the laundromat and shared that she had never owned a dishwasher. And yet, she impressed upon me the importance of perspective, noting the woman we had both seen hunched outside the door asking for money. *There are always people worse off,* she said. She also told me what gave her hope, like people and music and art.

Looking back, I am surprised by Mary's willingness to be vulnerable with a complete stranger. It makes me think of how lonely so many of us are, and how simple but significant it is to just look someone in the eyes and ask how they are doing.

I remember at one point she exclaimed, "I don't know why I'm telling you this!"

I probably just laughed, but there was something about her exclamation that marked me. It was a reminder of how sacred this moment was, in a world full of distraction and apathy. It didn't make logical sense for a woman to share these honest words with a stranger who was doing her homework on a Saturday night. But I am beginning to see how the moments that make life beautiful and oh-so-precious are not logical. They don't make sense, but they happen anyway, as if they are drawn out of us by grace and courage as we look at each other with love. It is these moments that remind me why I am here and why I wake up each day with hope, even though life can be so terribly heavy. It is a gift to behold someone for who they are, even if we have only known them for a short while, and to let them remind us of who we are. We too are worthy of love and care; we too have stories of resilience and hope worth sharing.

In his novel *The Moviegoer*, Walker Percy writes this stunning line: "I have discovered that most people have no one to talk to, no one, that is, who really wants to listen. When it does at last dawn on a man that you really want to hear about his business, the look that comes over his face is something to see."[3]

As I think about my conversation with Mary, Percy's words come to mind. It felt like a privilege to behold her. To listen and nod and say how sorry I was for the pain she had experienced. But I like to think that maybe I gave her something significant too. By listening to her—by slowing down and turning my focus from the tasks in my own little world—I was offering her my attention. And just maybe, the wonder that I experienced arose from seeing her realize that I really did care about her enough to lean all the way in.

It is amazing to be a part of something like that. Offering your attention to someone for free in a world that tries to monetize it is an incredible gift. It might not be convenient, and it certainly won't always be comfortable. But asking a stranger to let us peek into their world—and watching in amazement at what we see through the window—is worth being brave for. Time and time again, I have found this to be true.

The secret wisdom of strangers

Just as beholding someone allows us to give them the gift of our attention, it also creates space for us to receive a precious gift in return.

The next time you are standing in a crowded hallway, pause for a moment and look around you. Rotate slowly, taking it all in. The boy with the backpack that is bursting at the seams, the girl with blue hair and stylish ripped jeans, and the professor who is thumbing through a book, unaware of how close he is to knocking into someone. Consider how much life has been lived between all the souls who are squished in this space with you right now. Now expand your sphere of interest. Think about your school and your local community. There are so many people within your vicinity who carry remarkable stories, hard-won victories, and pearls of wisdom. But most of them, you just walk by.

A few months after meeting Helen at the reservoir, I saw her again while I was on an early morning run, and we decided to walk together. On this walk, we spoke of miracles, and she talked about losing her mother when she was just a few years older than I was. She also told me that our life is a song—which we can either express hate or extend love through. I tried to write all her wisdom down after we spoke because I wanted to internalize it.

What a profound opportunity I had to receive the gift of wisdom from somebody who had lived and lost, fallen and gotten back up again, only to find herself walking along a path that intersected mine for a moment. As we behold people, we are inviting them to speak into our lives. We are telling them that we want to carry their story with us as we move forward. Their story matters to more than just themselves; it matters to us too.

If I had seen Helen walking by me that initial spring day and chose not to engage with her, how much would I have missed out on? I probably would have formed a quick, inaccurate assumption about her life. And I never would have received the profound wisdom that she so freely shared with me.

The secret wisdom of strangers. Maybe it is not so secret after all—we are just too stuck in our own worlds to go looking for it. We chase around the same thoughts in our heads, trying to wrangle them. We run in circles but think we will end up somewhere new. We try to solve our problems ourselves, but we keep falling short.

Instead, if we are brave enough to reach out, we might be amazed by what we walk away with. Maybe a stranger's story of overcoming obstacles emboldens us to face our own trials with renewed grit. Maybe their account of a redeemed relationship inspires us to reach out to an estranged loved one. A stranger's wisdom may take the form of eloquently crafted gems they bestow upon us. Or it could simply lie tucked between the pages of their stories, and as they start to verbalize these pages, it is up to us to glean the wisdom they hold. Either way, if we listen closely, we may find the answers we are searching for. However unexpected our encounter was, suddenly we realize it was meant to be. Perhaps it was a divinely orchestrated encounter after all.

Reimagining beauty

As you think about this invitation to behold the strangers you meet, I want you to remember that it is more of a journey than a one-time decision. When life gets busy, the intention that we set to acknowledge the dignity of each person we pass may fall by the wayside. But that doesn't mean we can't retrieve it. Each time we leave our homes and head out into the mystery of the day that is still waiting to unfold, we can ask ourselves this question: *How can I see the people around me as art today?*

What is it about art that amazes us? How is it that a van Gogh masterpiece can have something in common with a middle schooler's drawing of a bowl of fruit? Well, I think it has something to do with our appreciation for its originality *and* its place in a wider collective of creative expressions. We begin to see the people before us as works of art when we can marvel at both their individuality *and* their intuitive connectedness to us. And in doing so, we get a chance to redeem our definition of beauty.

How easily we get carried away with our own definitions of beauty, especially in the college culture. We assume that beauty is synonymous with fashionable clothes, outward success, and perfection. The fewer blemishes something has, the more beautiful it is. Right? But what if we are missing a key component of beauty?

What if beauty looked more like authenticity than perfection? And what if beholding a person in their authenticity could be an act of celebration—a recognition of the beauty of life itself? Then just maybe, we would stop seeing the strangers we pass as mere inconveniences or disruptions to our well-laid plans. Instead, they would be recipients of this same glorious gift of life that we have received. And we would be in it together, all of us walking around with our unique footprints.

Can you imagine for a second that we each leave paint-stained footprints in our wake as evidence that we were here? Because that is what we all long for. To be noticed, to be known. For someone to see that we are here on this day, in this store, in line, or at the bus stop. And maybe, when the night falls upon this city where we wandered, we could take a special flashlight and see all the paint outlines of foot-prints. Red and blue and yellow and green. One of them belongs to you, and it is walking right beside another pair of footprints, circling the reservoir together, riding the campus bus, or slowly making their way through the textbook line.

Suddenly, you see that this creative act—this brave choice to engage with a stranger—makes you a part of the great art display of humankind: a living, breathing, ever-evolving masterpiece. We create art when we remember that we are in this human thing *together*. And choosing to look out for each other changes us. Because seeing another human—really seeing them—gives you new eyes to see yourself for the first time. *Beheld. Belonging. Beloved.*

CHAPTER 18

16 LITTLE SQUARES

On Being Heard

Dear resident,

Sitting at the fold out desk in front of my window, I glanced one last time around my pink childhood bedroom to check for stray socks sprawled across the floor. Then, I faced my computer, took a deep breath, and opened the Zoom link. After a brief period in the waiting room, I joined the meeting with unfamiliar faces popping up around me.

It was the first day of my creative nonfiction writing class. I signed up for the class on a whim during my last semester, after the creative writer in me had been dormant through most of my college career. As my professor Kim welcomed us to class, I immediately knew that I was in for something special.

For our first writing exercise, she asked us to create a timeline of significant events from our lives. But instead of simply naming moments, she instructed us to denote them with the sensory details they stirred up in our memories (like the smell of the doctor's gloves as they examined a broken arm or the taste of the chocolate cake at an uncle's wedding).

From that list, we chose one salient memory, put our pen to paper, and began writing about it. After 15 minutes, each person read an excerpt aloud to the group. I was amazed by the stories that my classmates shared. One of my classmates read a piece of philosophical musings from the point of view of his dog. Another student offered a poignant reflection on her hospitalization during a difficult season of her life. As I listened to them speak, I realized that my classmates' creative and vulnerable dispositions were rare. I could see that these were people who showed up with open hearts and non judgmental spirits. And I was confident that because of this vulnerability, our trust would only grow over the next few months.

After each person finished sharing, the rest of us unmuted ourselves, addressed the reader by name, and thanked them. As trust built, we were encouraged to add these seemingly simple words: "You are heard."

I loved hearing this chorus of voices, each one with their unique tone and rhythm, each one a reminder that I was not speaking into an empty void. But there were real people on the other end of that screen—real people who cared what I had to say.

David W. Augsburger said, "Being heard is so close to being loved that for the average person, they are almost indistinguishable."[1] When I remember what it felt like to sit in front of that computer screen with 15 pairs of eyes looking back at me, I know he is right.

Gratefully heard,
Elizabeth

We long to be heard

If we are being honest with ourselves, we could all hear these words a little more often: "You are heard." Underneath the masks we don and the armor we wear, we have hearts that ache to be heard. Maybe we have words on our tongues that we are afraid to say out loud, rooted in the lie that our stories are not as beautiful as our neighbors'. Or maybe we don't have all the words but would like some space to fumble around for them.

We long for a community that will hold us tenderly in silence and embrace us with joy when we are brave enough to fill it. But it can be hard to find a place where we feel safe sharing our words out loud. We live in a fast-moving, noisy world. In class, the cacophony of other voices might intimidate us. We might think: *Why do other students seem more confident than me when they answer a professor's question?* In our clubs, we may try to express our opinions, but our peers with more charisma may seem to overshadow us. *When will it be my turn to speak? When will my thoughts be valued equally? Do people even care what I have to say?*

The amazing thing about communities like the one I found in Kim's class is that they can surprise us. They remind us that our story matters when we have forgotten this for ourselves. **In a world full of noise, you are worthy of seeking out people who will hold space for you as you find your voice. We discover love not only by listening to others share their stories but also by being heard when we are ready to share ours.**

Scrolling squares

As the semester progressed, I came to adore this community we were forming. Amid loneliness, anxiety, and uncertainty about the future, I found a safe space where I could show up, completely and authentically myself. Each Monday morning at 11:00, I sat at my desk in anticipation. I was eager to turn on the camera, welcome people into my messy room and my messy life, and get a glimpse into theirs as well.

Those 16 squares knit us together across distances and differences. But when I think of squares that display the faces of my peers, most often I think of social media and how it does not always knit us together. Many of us enjoy expressing ourselves on social media. We share photos and videos from our lives and write captions to share our thoughts with others. Perhaps we feel like social media will fill this desire to be heard by others. But deep down, we know that this is not enough. The words and photos we share are likely buried between dozens of other posts that people are scrolling through. And a like or short comment will not make us feel like we have truly captured someone's attention. We long for more. We long to be listened to.

Since I started sharing my writing publicly, I have found it easier to write something and put it out into the world without considering who will read it. Sometimes, I am too focused on making the words sound eloquent. Or I am afraid of receiving criticism. But while it may feel safer to protect myself from external opinions, there is no greater feeling as a writer than hearing how my words have impacted someone for the better. And to do this, I must be willing to "be heard."

We regularly fall into this trap on social media too. Instead of reaching out to a group of friends and sharing the words that are in our hearts, we release a post into the world, hoping that our followers will interact with it in some way. We dampen the opportunity to *be heard* by real people whose stories may be similar to ours. We reduce each other to the screens we scroll on instead of the individuals these screens belong to. We forget the gifts of holding someone's attention, of being cared for, of knowing that we matter to someone. In Sherry Turkle's words, "Face-to-face conversation is the most human—and humanizing—thing we do. Fully present to one another, we learn to listen. It's where we develop the capacity for empathy. It's where we experience the joy of being heard, of being understood."[2]

What's my story anyway?

I have always been an avid journaler. If you open my closet, you will see a chest that houses journals from my high school and college years—hundreds of pages containing snippets as ordinary as what I ate for dinner to confessions as serious as my fears about the future. And in another box, you will find notebooks from my childhood years with recollections that really ran the gamut. From describing a painful ear infection to blaming my brother for the timeout I was in to listing all the Disney Channel shows I watched—no detail was too trivial for little Elizabeth to record.

When the pandemic first hit, I started a new notebook to record my experiences from that momentous era in history. At first, I was excited. But as the days all started to blend together, the ink ran dry. *If the story outside the page held little interest to me, why should I bother to record it?* Maybe I was cynical. Perhaps I had a case of the "pandemic blues." Whatever the cause, Kim's class turned out to be the cure.

One of my "aha moments" from that class was that I did not have to just write about my present experiences. Instead, I could dive into my past, pulling out stories I had long since forgotten. I could be a historian, a time traveler, and a treasure hunter.

Kim's advice from the first day of class—to tie a memory to a specific sensory experience—continued to impact my writing throughout the semester. It was a powerful experience to viscerally access the moments that had a part in shaping who I had become, for better and for worse. This practice kept me honest in my recollection. And although our memories will always be flawed, I am learning just how important our best efforts at honesty are in this process of retrieving memories and pulling them back to the present.

Rather than trying to write "my story" all at once, I spent the semester piecing together memories of moments that felt significant. Some were seemingly ordinary moments that captured a particular feeling—like being safe and loved. Others were moments of extreme heartache or elation. I don't think it is fair to assume that we have only "one story" to share. Just as we must be careful not to adopt a "single story" to understand others, we must also resist the temptation to overidentify with one story we have lived. Our lives are made up of countless stories. Sure, there may be significant themes weaving through them. But ultimately, we are endlessly complex beings, unable to be reduced to simple narratives.

The gift of silence

In almost every writing class that semester, we took time to tilt our cameras toward our notebooks, sit in silence, and just write. Kim told us to never stop moving our pens. At first, her request scared me. But over time, it was freeing.

Each time we found ourselves writing what was "expected of us," Kim was there to remind us of a better way. She asked us to look deeper—to write not just what we thought but also what we felt. To let all that was within us make its way onto the page—a canvas waiting to soak in the "emotional heat" that had been rising in us. For some of us, it was simmering. For others, it had been ready to burst for quite a while.

I don't think we realized how much we needed to unlearn about writing. We were so used to creating outlines and formulating words based on how we assumed they should sound, rather than how they would feel coming out of us. Kim encouraged us to search for truer words. She reminded us that we write not only to tell a reader what we believe but also to bring them on our journey of discovery. And this journey begins with sitting in silence and letting the words reveal themselves to us.

To be honest, even though I have encouraged you to practice accepting silence, like when speaking to a stranger, I have always been uncomfortable with it. I am quick to speak when conversations lull. Sometimes, I say things that sound silly or unnecessary so I can avoid an awkward silence. And yet, I am beginning to see silence for the gift that it is.

There is a particular kind of silence that allows us to sift around in the dark for a while and familiarize ourselves with the color of light again. It is a silence that cannot be forced or rushed. It must not be thrust upon us, begging us to fill it before we are ready. When we find ourselves in this silence, all the small talk and filler words we usually default to trickle away. And as we lose these safety nets, we learn to truly listen and be listened to. We learn to receive and be received.

In Kim's class, this time of writing in silence allowed us to greet the most authentic versions of ourselves—the ones that emerged as we moved our pens and quieted our minds; the ones that climbed out when the noise of the world fell away. We could just be. And from that quiet place, we could find the courage to retrieve the words we needed to speak out loud.

Holding space

As I found the courage to share parts of my story with my classmates, I was grateful to be met with such genuine care and interest. This experience showed me how much I craved the words: "You are heard." I craved them because I felt lonely and because it is so easy to forget what is true about ourselves when the lies in our heads are loud. I craved them because I know how rare they are in this loud world.

When others hold space for us, they remind us that we possess something special—not only words worth speaking but also words worth listening to. When we watch their eyes light up or see their heads nod with understanding, we know that they are receiving us as we are. And just maybe, they are connecting to a piece of our story.

Looking back, I still marvel at the gift I received in that class. It was evident that my classmates wanted to listen to me because they loved me *and* they cared about the particulars of what I said. Both are important: believing we are worthy of being listened to *and* believing that the words we speak have value.

Ultimately, over the course of that semester, my classmates helped me remember what I had forgotten when I stopped writing journal entries at the beginning of the pandemic. In case you have forgotten it too, dear reader, I will say it to you now: *Your words matter. Your story matters. And your life matters.*

Practical tips for holding space with your own community

So, what are the attributes of a community that shows up to listen, learn, and respond when appropriate? Are these experiences only possible in rare moments, or could they be more common than we think?

While I cannot tell you exactly how to cultivate these communities in your particular circumstances, I can share a few characteristics of our writing community. You may notice that this advice echoes encouragement from previous chapters when I spoke about the *Everybody, Always* group and my RA staff. Rather than being a brand-new experience for me, this class was a reminder of what I had already been learning about building communities on my college journey:

- **Connect over shared pain:** For us, this looked like having to navigate unfamiliar terrain attending college during a disruptive pandemic. For you, this may look like joining a support group for grief or participating in a fundraiser for a cause that has impacted your life.

- **Connect over shared joy:** We all had a different relationship with writing, but each one of us got to rekindle the joy of putting pen to paper and watching words form out of thin air. For you, this could look like joining a service program with an attached small group reflection component.

- **Size matters:** While we don't want to be exclusive, there is value in being vulnerable in a smaller setting. If many of your classes take place in large lecture halls, consider signing up for a smaller seminar.

- **Building trust takes time:** Don't pressure yourself or other group members to rush this process. It is a gift to watch people open up more and more over time.

- **Choose courage:** In Brené Brown's wise words, "Vulnerability is not winning or losing; it's having the courage to show up and be seen when we have no control over the outcome. Vulnerability is not weakness; it's our greatest measure of courage."[3]

Sounds like love

In one of the last classes of the semester, I decided to read aloud a deeply personal story I had written a few days prior. It was not elegant; it was raw and vulnerable. But if I had learned anything over the previous few months, it was the power of speaking words of truth and letting them pull us closer to others.

I read my story with a few intermittent voice cracks, staring down at my paper because I was frightened to imagine having an audience for this story (yes, I know that seems antithetical to the point of this chapter, but I am only human). I made my way through the words on the page slowly but steadily. When I finished reading, I felt my face burning and wondered if my classmates could see the red blotches forming on my pale chest. I took a deep breath and glanced up from the page. That's when I saw 15 little squares filled with beautiful faces who had deep love in their eyes.

I didn't need them to say the words, but they did anyway.

"Elizabeth, you are heard."

And I was.

CHAPTER 19

A CONNECTICUT THANKSGIVING

On Coming Home

If you are an incoming college student, some of the questions that I pose in this chapter will not yet be relevant to you. You can return to these questions when you arrive on campus.

Dear resident,

We were walking to White Mountain, the popular ice cream shop across from campus, when my friend Anna invited me to spend Thanksgiving with her family in Connecticut. It was two months into my freshman year, and I had recently met Anna through our church community. I had never met her family nor been to Connecticut before. But when she heard that I was unsure if I could fly 3,000 miles home for a few days, she responded with that gracious invitation.

I was flooded with a range of emotions as I pondered her words; honestly, my feelings swung back and forth between anxiety, gratitude, uncertainty, and anticipation. But before I could think about what this would entail, I responded enthusiastically, "That would be amazing!"

So, two weeks later, I was loading my giant red duffle bag into her sister's car. Although the trip was only four days long, I looked like I had packed for four months. You don't have to be a genius to guess why—I was overcompensating for all the unknowns that long weekend would bring.

Over the next few days, Anna brought me along as she weaved back into the rhythms of home, a place she was returning to for the first time in a few months. And somehow, I seemed to fit into her routine, even though I wasn't from there. I wondered what it was like for her to have a friend tag along on her first trip home since going to college. If she was annoyed or regretting her decision, she didn't show it.

Anna took me along to her favorite diner as we met up with her high school friend. I shopped with her mom at Old Navy as she worked at the cash register. We went to her church where I sang softly, surrounded by a chorus of beautiful voices, and she introduced me to the sweet elderly man with whom she counted Christmas trees on the roofs of cars each year. We ran the Turkey Trot on Thanksgiving Day in 28 °F weather and sat around the campfire as her closest friends shared their adventures at their respective colleges. In between these interactions, she explained inside jokes and nicknames and little secrets about her town, which was becoming more precious to me each day.

Growing up on the West Coast, everything felt exciting to me about this new town: the Long Island Sound, mulled apple cider at a local café, the gazebo in the park that reminded me of the one from *Gilmore Girls*, and the house with the Christmas light display that I suspected ran up a hefty energy bill (though it was a marvel to gaze upon).

But the best part of the trip was the way that Anna welcomed me into her family. I remember standing on her front porch assembling a puzzle with her aunt, mom, and grandma. Circling the neighborhood with her grandfather as the golden leaves shimmered in the sunlight and crunched under our feet. And sitting around the table for our Thanksgiving meal, enjoying delicious food and the blessing of being together.

During my sophomore year, I went back to Anna's for Thanksgiving and Easter too. Each time, I was welcomed back into a town and a family I had come to love. It was certainly a gift that I had not anticipated when I first said yes to Anna's invitation.

Though it has been a few years since I've traveled to Connecticut, when I think of Thanksgiving, I think of Fairfield. I think of marshmallows on sticky fingers around the campfire, Anna's famous cranberry sauce, her sister's homemade mac and cheese, her brother's love of *Jeopardy!*, her mom's beautiful singing voice, and the prayer that we shared before our meal as our hearts filled with gratitude.

Gratefully welcomed in,
Elizabeth

Expanding our view of home

The long weekend in Connecticut was the first of many occasions that contributed to my shifting perspective of "home" while I was in college. When I first arrived at school, home felt like an anchor when everything was new and unknown. There was an invisible string stretching from Boston back to my hometown in California, and I followed it (usually over the phone, sometimes with my body) when I felt lost or sad or afraid. But over time, I expanded my view of "home."

I know the adage, "There's no place like home," and I certainly understand the sentiment. Home can be the house where you took your first steps and ran around with paint on your fingertips, hearing your mom's stern voice telling you not to mark the walls. But home can also be forged in new places; it can be found in the spaces that hold us on our journeys of becoming. The sensation of comfort and sense of belonging attached to home can move with us wherever we go. We can plant deep roots even in temporary seasons, for they are not dependent on the location of the soil but rather on the people who plant them with us.

I want to invite you to reflect on your current perspective of home. *Is it limited to the walls that sheltered you as you grew up? Do you only let yourself find rest and recovery for your body when you can settle into this specific place? What might you be missing out on with this narrow definition? And who might you be missing the chance to extend hospitality to and receive it from?*

As you think about your college journey and your life beyond college, I hope you too will come to find "home" in unexpected places. **"Home" can be the places where people open their doors to us, giving us space to unload the burdens on our backs. And we discover love as we accept these gracious extensions of hospitality that give** us space to recover, connect with others, and have our tangible needs met in unique ways.

Leaving home

Before we enter a new home, we must be willing to step out of the old one. For some of us, this is easy. The older we get, the more eager we are to depart from the nest. We want to throw off anything that hinders us from embarking on the adventures we dream of. We are ready to swing open the door, prance down the steps, and jump into whatever mode of transportation will deliver us to our new destination. We are one bird duet away from embodying a Disney princess in a castle, singing her way to freedom.

But for others, this is one of the scariest decisions we will ever make. As I think back to myself at eighteen, I am amazed at the courage I displayed in choosing a college so far from home. If I was sick, my mom wouldn't be able to take care of me. If I was missing my family, I couldn't just drive home for the weekend. Wherever you find yourself, whether 3 miles or 3,000 miles from home, know that it was an act of courage to leave the place you considered home and settle somewhere new. There are so many unknowns when we first arrive somewhere: What will the rooms smell like? What will the food taste like? Will the neighbors be friendly, indifferent, or rude?

If we give up so much when we venture away from the place we call home, is it worth it? Why should we leave behind the comforts of home to step into so many unknowns? For me, the answer lies not only in the wondrous sights I might see but also in the people I might encounter. From the glimpse you have had into my life, imagine how many friendships, connections, and memorable experiences I would have missed out on if I had never taken that leap and flown to Boston. Now think about the adventures you could experience. Do they feel like something worth risking the unknowns for?

This chapter might resonate with you in several ways. If you are just beginning your time at college, I challenge you to give this new place a chance. Sometimes, leaving home is not just a physical step we take but also an internal decision we make. In no way do I want you to let go of the ties you have to home, like meaningful phone calls with your parents or friends from high school. But I have seen how easy it can be to close ourselves off from our new home, clutching so tightly to the home we miss that it is as if we never really left.

Homesickness is natural. It is nothing to be embarrassed about, and adjusting to a new environment takes time. But sometimes, the best way to move past the fear is to bravely step into the new community in which we find ourselves, leaning in and letting our curiosity lead us toward others, believing we are worthy of more than settling for loneliness and self-sufficiency. The gift of this new home is that we get to learn how to live alongside new people; in doing so, we might come to see ourselves as belonging to a collective greater than ourselves. And in this collective, we awaken to the beauty of interdependence and vulnerability.

On the flip side, maybe you have been at college for a while and this is the place you refer to as home. That is wonderful! Embrace this version of home and savor the parts that make it unique. But be careful not to ignore opportunities to continue moving out of your comfort zone. Whether it means welcoming new classmates into your dorm for meaningful conversations, visiting friends at their new apartments, traveling to new cities, or even starting to consider your post grad plans, give yourself the gift of experiencing life beyond the comforts of one particular home. The world is full of new places to explore—and we can find sanctuary in the most unexpected places.

Knock on the door

Like many of the transformations I have invited you to consider in these chapters, the first step is not some huge act but a fairly simple one. Knock on the door.

I remember one door I knocked on during my time studying abroad that will always fill me with a sense of wonder. On a trip to Norway, I drove with two friends from the city of Oslo to a cabin in the mountains. As we drove, the changes in scenery mimicked the passing of seasons. We saw beautiful lakes, fields, and trees speckled across mountains. And as we made our way higher and higher, we passed a light dusting of snow that quickly evolved into a thick blanket. I was so caught up in the scenery that I hardly noticed a cabin sitting atop a steep driveway after a bend in the road.

My Norwegian friend exclaimed, "There's an *open* sign on the door!" Suddenly, she turned the car off the road and took us up the driveway. There sat a quaint wooden home overlooking the mountains with a pointed roof and a red door. "Are you sure there is a shop here?" I asked skeptically. It was hard to imagine someone operating one in such a rural area. My friend, however, was insistent and walked to the side door to ring the doorbell. After a few moments, a kind woman answered and told us that she indeed had a café in her house. She pointed to the front entrance and said we were more than welcome to come in.

We entered a small room with a beautiful antique shelving unit that held a variety of teas. The woman had long graying hair, a strong stature, and a warm smile. We took a seat at the counter, and when we realized that the tea was home grown, we ordered a pot and bought some bags of leaves to enjoy later. I savored the best honey I had ever tasted, admired the sheepskins that were cushions for our chairs, and watched my friend chat cheerfully with the woman in Norwegian. My friend explained that she didn't have many customers at this time, so it was special for us to take time to be with her.

When we asked to use the restroom, she let us into her own home! Standing in her living room, we admired wooden furniture pieces carved by her ancestors and looked on as she proudly showed us photos of her children growing up. She then led us onto her back porch where we stood in awe—the view of the mountains was stunning. We thanked our host for her hospitality before heading back to the car, where we all echoed sentiments of gratitude.

While this may be a unique example, it reminds me how much is hidden behind the doors that we pass by. From the outside, we often do not know what lies behind a closed door. But once inside, we can find something incredible.

At college, I enjoyed meeting up with friends in all sorts of places— dining halls, libraries, cafés, classrooms after hours, and on wooden benches in the springtime. But there was something special about gathering in a person's dorm room or off-campus house. When we knock on the door and someone invites us in, we get a glimpse into the space they inhabit. And most often, these spaces reflect our values, what we find beautiful, and even who we aspire to be outside these walls.

At first glance, we may notice how tidy (or untidy) a room is. Maybe we observe how the occupant spends their time (studying or relaxing or making art). But when we look a little closer, we might see reflections of the person before us. As I have shared, the more we learn about a person's story—the more we come to truly *know* them—the greater our opportunity is to cultivate love for them.

What do the doors look like that you have shied away from knocking on? Maybe you have felt lonely but walked by your RA's door, hesitating because you didn't want to bother them. Perhaps a new friend invited you over for dinner, but you struggled to find time in your busy schedule. These reasons are understandable, but I hope you will overcome your hesitancy. Because after we knock on the door, we may get the chance to receive the gift of hospitality.

The gift of receiving hospitality

If you are like me, sometimes it is difficult for you to receive hospitality. We live in a culture that promotes self-sufficiency. We enjoy providing for ourselves and are reluctant to ask for help. But when we step into someone else's home, we are in a new element. The comforts of our own homes are replaced by unfamiliar spaces. And so, we must rely on the generosity of the host to meet our needs.

Renowned poet and memoirist Kathleen Norris said, "True hospitality is marked by an open response to the dignity of each and every person."[1] What a marvelous definition. I love how her words emphasize the warm reception of the host toward the guest, rather than the appearance of the home. When we receive hospitality, we give ourselves the chance to be cared for in a tangible way. And deep down, we yearn for someone to remind us that we are worthy of receiving this kind of love.

Not only does another person's hospitality bless us, but when we gratefully receive it, they are blessed as well. I recall Rosa, the host mom of my residencia in Spain. She cared for us in so many practical ways, like washing our laundry and cooking our meals. But she also cared for our spirits. I still remember the absolute joy on her face when she celebrated students' birthdays with a festive song blasting from her portable speakers. She showed us that she loved the role she played in our lives, making us feel cherished so far from home.

The homes that we are welcomed into are like the benches that lined the reservoir where I sat when I was weary or just wanted to take a moment to marvel at the view—they always gave me rest. When I wanted to sink into the beauty around me and let it transform me or quietly observe people passing by, they held me. In those times, the benches found me, letting me come home to myself for a while.

The best homes do this. They welcome us to be ourselves, even as we are transformed by the people around us. They give us space in the little nooks and crannies to find moments of silence to hear our own desires and needs. They give us time to rest as we unload the heavy burdens we have been carrying. And they call us back to the people we gather with—to remember that somehow, we can find ourselves and lose ourselves at the same time, caught up in this *togetherness*.

What might it look like for you to receive hospitality? In the previous chapter, I invited you to discover love as others honor your voice. In this chapter, I hope you will allow people to care for your body. Hospitality is not a one-size-fits-all practice. There may be many ways that the people in your life seek to meet your needs when you are a guest in their home. But my sincere hope is that each experience will remind you that you are worthy of being cared for. And the more you learn this, the more you will want to extend this gift to others.

Practice simple hospitality

One evening, a few months after we had met, I ran into my friend Noah as I was walking across campus after a football game. It was a cold, rainy November evening and we were both soaked. I invited him to my dorm to dry off. When we arrived at my small dorm room, he told me that his socks were soaked and asked if he could dry them with my hair dryer. I grabbed my purple hair dryer and handed it to him. He sat on the carpet, pulled his socks off, and began drying them. I can't help but laugh when I recall that memory. It was such a funny sight to behold—but it was also kind of wonderful.

That memory is a reminder of how simple hospitality can be. We don't need to overthink it. Sometimes, all we need to do is provide our friends with a warm place to rest and dry off after a rainy day. There is something about the small act of meeting someone's tangible needs that strengthens our connection to them and reminds us that we are not that different after all.

As you are getting to know people in your dorm, classes, clubs, and faith communities, how can you practice simple hospitality? We may not have as much to offer our friends as we would like (let's just say that a tiny dorm room is not the best place to host a dinner party). But we can offer them what we have—a warm place to rest, a jar of candy, a microwaved mug of tea, and even a hairdryer. As we welcome others into our space, we get to show them an unadorned piece of our lives. It might sound minor, but as we let our guard down for others, it can give them the courage to do the same.

Think of someone you are just getting to know. Is there a classmate you are working on a project with who you always meet in the library? What if you invited them back to your dorm room, or your dorm lounge if you would feel more comfortable there? How might you extend the act of simple hospitality to them?

I fondly remember the many times I welcomed people into my dorm room—new friends, old friends, residents, and other RAs. There is something disarming about letting others see our more human side—the photos we choose to decorate our walls with, the laundry basket hidden in the corner, the bowl we microwave oatmeal in when we are running late and can't make it to the dining hall in the morning. This authenticity allows us to connect in a deeper way, beyond the surface-level conversations that we often default to.

Practical ways I designed my dorm room for hospitality:

- I set up the space for gathering comfortably with a couch, rugs on the floor, and a little table.

- I placed jars of candy on my shelf for residents who wanted a treat.

- I had a collection of mugs on my windowsill and a container of tea bags for "tea nights" dedicated to meaningful conversation.

- I decorated for holidays so that both my guests and I could find joy in the delights of small, beautiful things.

- I bought bright flowers at a local grocery store and displayed them in a mason jar.

Making a home at college

For better or worse, our time at college does not last forever. It only lasts for a period; hopefully one that is brimming with meaning, hope, and love. But if our residence is temporary, is it still possible to enjoy the gifts of home here? I have come to believe that it is.

I want to invite you to reflect on the home you are making at college. But instead of just thinking about it, what would it be like to feel it? After all, "home" is more about a feeling we experience than the physical space we inhabit.

First, listen. What are the sounds that comfort you when you step foot on campus after a break or return to your dorm room after a weekend away? Is it the ringing of the church bells on Sunday morning? Is it the purr of the elevator, the echoes of coughs in the library, the plucking of tenacious fingers on a keyboard in class, or the giggles drifting under your door from your friends down the hall?

Now, look. What do you see now that you have lived in this place and made it your home? What do you notice that a prospective student on a tour would not recognize? Do you spot the snakelike shape of the line in the dining hall at 2 p.m.? Do you see the turkeys outside your dorm window in the fall, brazenly roaming free?

What do you smell? The "old book" smell emanating from the shelves of your favorite library and your roommate's famous brownies baking in the oven?

What do you taste? Vending machine Skittles at 1 a.m., chocolate croissants from the café between classes, mint tea in your best friend's mug?

Finally, what can you touch? Cool air hitting your skin when you walk into the ice hockey arena, blades of grass brushing your feet as you walk across campus in sandals during spring, the firm cinder block wall against your back as you sit crisscross applesauce in the dorm hallway, chatting with your friends and greeting passersby?

Begin with your senses. When your mind is spinning and your emotions run wild, return to your senses. You can trust them. You will feel in your body that this is home, likely before your mind catches up to it. We long to feel safe, to find refuge from a hostile world. Even if we are tempted to idealize this concept of home, deep down we know it won't be perfect. But we don't need it to be perfect. We just need it to feel like home. We want to be comfortable enough to take our socks off, let our guards down, bare our souls to the moon as we wander the campus at night, and let out a deep breath when we finally crawl into our beds at the end of a long day.

It might sound strange for me to say that I fell in love with a place. And yet, that is exactly what I did. Because a place is more than a location with GPS coordinates on a map. This place, Boston College, was the soil upon which I grew over the course of four years. It was a warm haven during snowstorms and a cool reprieve on humid August days. It is a place where cafés and libraries still echo with the words I said to my friends when the night held us gently. Its stone walls hold memories of joy and heartache, courage and disappointment. And outside those walls, the welcome kiss of spring or the fresh fall air carried me on long runs over hills and around reservoirs, as my worries slid away for a little while.

That feeling of coming home—it is something that we all long for. I hope you are open now to the idea that we can find it in more than one place. I felt it when we spent time with Anna's grandparents. As we greeted her grandfather at the door of his retirement community, he hugged each of his grandkids, then he hugged me. I felt it in Sevilla whenever I returned from a weekend trip and walked up the stairs in Rosa's residencia, where I was greeted by the familiar sounds of laughter and silverware clinking against dishes. I felt it whenever I drove through the tunnel between Boston Logan Airport and campus. As I emerged from the darkness, I lifted my eyes to the familiar skyline and smiled, filled with a mixture of excitement and tranquility.

This too is home.

I still have that anchor back to my home in California. But it is not alone anymore. It is connected to other ropes with smaller anchors. *Fairfield, Connecticut, and Sevilla, Spain, and Chestnut Hill, Massachusetts.* These were the places where I grew up and the places that grew me. The places where I learned to love and be loved—and where I realized that there is no greater pursuit in life than this.

CHAPTER 20

A GRADUATION TO REMEMBER

On Being Loved

Dear resident,

I watched the sun begin its descent in the distance. The vast emptiness of the Nevada desert stretched out for miles, and a growing sense of dread festered inside me. *I am not safe here. I need to go home. Now.*

Mom and I were pulled over on the side of the road, seven hours into our seven-day road trip from California to Massachusetts. After spending my senior year at home, I was planning to drive to my college graduation. I told myself that the panic symptoms would be less severe by car than by plane. But I quickly found that traveling even a small distance from home felt overwhelming.

Suddenly, there I was in the middle of nowhere with a decision to make: continue or abandon our plan and drive back home.

I stared out into the open landscape, hoping to find the strength to continue. Hoping to find peace about a journey to one of my favorite places in the world to see the people I loved. That was worth finding the courage to persevere, right?

Instead, all I found was fear.

"Okay, let's turn around."

"Are you sure?" I could hear the sadness in Mom's voice— not for her, but for me.

I nodded. "Yeah, I'm sure."

She hopped into the driver's seat and began the long drive home. As the sky darkened, my body began shaking, searing pain gripped my stomach, and my head throbbed. This was panic at its most brutal. I prayed for mercy the whole ride home.

When we finally arrived home, I felt great relief. But soon after, I was left with disappointment. By giving into fear, I believed I had let myself down. And even worse, I had let my friends down. I had let down everyone who I promised I would find my way back to after so many months of separation. I was a girl who valued relationships above all else. And yet, I wasn't strong enough to keep driving forward.

With disappointment,
Elizabeth

Graduation day

I woke up on graduation day, slipped into the black robe and cap that were hanging in my closet, and stood in front of my wall mirror.

My face looked tired and void of make up. Why bother with it? It would just be my parents and me watching the ceremony on our television. It was so different than I imagined when I first walked down Linden Lane at convocation.

The ceremony began at 7 a.m. California time. My parents and I sank into our couch, cushions sagging beneath us, with breakfast on our laps. I enjoyed listening to the commencement address and watching the procession of my classmates through our football stadium. But it felt so strange to be absent. When I walked across my family room to receive a blank piece of paper from my mom, it just didn't feel the same as a stage.

Then I got a text from my uncle who lived an hour away, asking if he could come by to congratulate me. When he walked through the front door, he held pink balloons that commemorated my academic achievement. There was something special about celebrating this milestone with my family, who supported me throughout my academic journey. The people who celebrate us, even when we feel less than our best, remind us that life doesn't have to be perfect before we honor the strides we have made to get to where we are.

The next surprise arrived at my front door wrapped in a green ribbon. It was a bouquet of beautiful flowers with a note from two of my earliest college friends. We had all lived on the same floor freshman year. Now, four years later, amid all the craziness of graduation week, they took the time to ensure that this gorgeous gift would arrive at my door 3,000 miles away. I didn't have the words to express just how much that meant to me.

The last surprise came from my brother Steven as he FaceTimed me from Brooklyn that evening. He sent me a link to a website with videos, photos, and written messages from my community. I smiled from ear to ear as I received heartfelt messages from friends, classmates, former teachers, neighbors, and family members. They shared attributes they admired in me and memories we had made together. Whatever beliefs I had about disappointing myself and others faded into the background. This college journey—although it was ending so differently than I had wished—was filled to the brim with meaning, hope, and love.

I fell asleep that night with a deep sense of gratitude. I wanted to show up for the people in my life, but instead, they showed up for me. When I felt my sense of connection slipping away, they took the time to remind me of the precious communities I was a part of. But more importantly, when I saw myself as a failure, they reminded me who I was. I was so loved.

Loved in my weakness

That day was a reminder of what I had come to learn throughout my time at college: **It is in the moments when we feel weak and broken that the people who love us show up in profound and beautiful ways. It is when we are at our worst when we finally see the truth: our constant pursuit of success and improvement only hinders us from receiving the gift of grace—being loved for who we are, not what we do.**

How often do I place my sense of worth in fickle things? How often do I believe I am worthier of love when I greet life's challenges with courage?

Losing the capabilities and confidence I once took pride in forced me to present myself to others with less of a facade, to admit that I was more vulnerable than I ever imagined. And just maybe, I needed people to hold me up when I couldn't brave the storms of life on my own.

The way Mom took care of me when I felt like my body was breaking. The way my friends FaceTimed me before graduation so I could get a glimpse of the festivities. My uncle's visit, my friends' gorgeous flowers, and my brother's heartfelt gift. Every extension of love toward me when I felt unworthy was a balm.

The circumstances that led to these encounters with grace and compassion were not what I would have wished for—and yet they carved out space for love to fill in the holes that fear had burrowed into my life. They enabled me to be a witness to undeserved kindness and a recipient of intentional generosity.

When we try to earn love, we fall short time and time again. But when we confess that we are struggling, we choose authenticity over illusion—and we give the people around us the chance to love us just as we are.

You are loved

As we come to the end of our journey together, I couldn't think of a better story to share with you than the day I graduated.

Of course, it feels appropriate to end a book about college with graduation. But more than that, the events that happened on this day—big and small—reminded me of my belovedness. And above all, that is what I want to leave you with.

Friend, you are so loved. Not after you have proven your worth or accomplished a goal, but right in the middle of your messy feelings, unmet longings, and moments of weakness. Surround yourself with people who remind you of this. And just maybe, you can be that person for someone else.

YOU'LL KNOW IT
WHEN YOU FEEL IT

Y ou'll know it when you feel it.

Marina Keegan called it "the opposite of loneliness."

In 2012, Keegan published a beautiful essay with this title in the *Yale Daily News* the week of her graduation. She died tragically in a car accident later that week.

In her essay, she described this feeling she found at college: "It's not quite love and it's not quite community; it's just this feeling that there are people, an abundance of people, who are in this together. Who are on your team. When the check is paid and you stay at the table. When it's four a.m. and no one goes to bed. That night with the guitar. That night we can't remember. That time we did, we went, we saw, we laughed, we felt. The hats."[1]

The week of my graduation, I reread her essay and sent it to my friends. Her words resonated deeply with me.

I left my college suddenly, unexpectedly, when the world shut down—and I graduated 3,000 miles away. I lost 1.5 years in a place I had come to love more than I could have imagined, filled with people who all hold pieces of my heart as they walk around living their beautiful lives on the many paths that life has taken us.

And yet I knew *it*. I can confidently say that I knew the feeling. And I hold on to it tightly when I need a reminder that I am not alone in this world.

My prayer for you is that you will experience the gift of feeling it too.

That college will not just be a place where you walk a straight path looking at the ground, fill out answers on tests, and walk away with a piece of paper. I want you to walk off the path when a beautiful conversation catches your ear. I want you to keep asking questions of yourself and the people around you, and to never lose wonder for the beauty this life holds. I want you to laugh through the times when life feels beautiful and lean on the people who love you when it feels terrifying.

I hope you remember the words I have shared about discovering meaning and moving forward with hope and embracing opportunities to be transformed by love.

And I hope these four years will give you a chance to experience the feeling that Marina felt and that I felt too. Maybe you will experience it for the first time. And like me, you will realize that you want to chase it for the rest of your life.

"For me, it was always going to be about love."[2]

May it be so.

ACKNOWLEDGMENTS

When I began writing this book, I stuck a note to my binder that read, "I want to create something beautiful with and for the people I love." What a gift it is to see this dream come to fruition. I would like to thank the people who supported me on this incredible journey.

Mom, thank you for being my sounding board, my patient encourager, and my first reader. Dad, thank you for dreaming with me, letting my excitement be your excitement, and inspiring me to step into uncertainty with courage. Steven, thank you for cheering me on from across the country and being my proud big brother. And thank you to my extended family for all your love.

I am unbelievably grateful for my writing group—Cristi Schroeder, Jess Henning, and Erin Michele Smith. How far we have come together since God placed us in that Hope*Writers breakout group two years ago. Thank you for your encouragement, wisdom, passion, and prayers.

To my dear friends who read my chapters along the way and offered thoughtful feedback—Josie Seelen, Kyle Rosenthal, Caroline King, Ellie Roberts, John Zulewski, Rachel Van Boxtel, Catherine Schofield, Sara Knapp, Mary Kenney, Anna Fedoryk, Sarah Ashebir, Laura Rodrigues, Jill Pruner, Taylor Kay, Martha McGee, Lee Hartley, and Darrah Garvin. Thank you for generously giving your time, honesty, encouragement, and ideas for improvement. Hearing how my words impacted you—even in their unpolished form—inspired me to keep writing.

To my editors and designer—Laurie Chittenden, Ameesha Green, Christina Roth, and Steve Kuhn. Thank you for going above and beyond to help me create a book I am immensely proud of. You have been a joy to work with.

Thank you to my residents for making me an RA. I am honored that you trusted me to walk alongside you through laughter-filled days and tender moments. Each day in Loyola Two was a gift.

To Kim Garcia and our beautiful writing class—thank you for helping me fall in love with the craft of writing again. Thank you for holding space as I found the courage to tell the stories that matter to me.

I am so grateful to the people in my Boston College community who made the stories in this book possible. I would especially like to thank my professors, my faith community, the *Everybody, Always* group, the PULSE program, the Jenks Leadership Program, the CLXF staff, Kelsey Werner, Becca Francesconi, Will Johnson, Nick Alvarez, Noah Jussila, and Maddy Van Husen.

I was blessed to have wonderful cheerleaders as I wrote this book. Christine Pimlott, thank you for reading my messy drafts and sharing enthusiastic and insightful feedback. Jill Olson, thank you for believing in me from the very beginning of this writing journey and continuing to offer me support. Lisa Otsuka, thank you for teaching me how to stay awake to the world around me, write honest words, and live wholeheartedly. You have all blessed me immensely with your wisdom, sincerity, and encouragement.

Thank you to the Jensen family for showing me how friends can become family. After a day of writing or editing, there was nothing better than walking through your front door and playing with my beloved goddaughter.

To my friend Jesus—thank you for your hope in the darkest of times, your love in my weakness, and your joy as we pursued this great adventure together.

NOTES

Preface

1. *About Time*, directed by Richard Curtis (Los Angeles: Universal Pictures, 2013), 2:03:00, https://tv.apple.com/us/movie/about-time/umc.cmc.2vfd635fg0hxxlsqcetlzw8mp.

Introduction

1. Kate Bowler, "Arthur Brooks: When Success Isn't Success," September 19, 2022, in *Everything Happens with Kate Bowler*, podcast, 45:37, https://katebowler.com/podcasts/arthur-brooks-when-success-isnt-success/.

2. Bowler, "Arthur Brooks."

Chapter 1

1. G. K. Chesterton, *Tremendous Trifles* (New York: Dodd, Mead and Company, 1909), 7, https://www.google.com/books/edition/_/3KUEAQAAIAAJ?hl=en&gbpv=0.

2. "Improving Her Depression, Woman Tries Something New Every Day for a Year—And Vows to Keep It Up," *Good News Network*, January 3, 2023, https://www.goodnewsnetwork.org/depressed-woman-tried-something-new-every-day-for-a-year/.

3. Mary Oliver, "The Summer Day," in *New and Selected Poems*, vol. 1 (Boston: Beacon Press, 1992), 94.

4. Sacred Ordinary Days, accessed January 29, 2023, https://sacredordinarydays.com/.

5. *1 Second Everyday Diary*, v. 4.9.3 (1 Second Everyday, P.B.C., 2013), iOS 15.0 or later.

6. Anne Lamott, *Bird by Bird: Some Instructions on Writing and Life*, 2nd Anchor Books ed. (New York: Anchor Books, 2019), 94.

7. *The Perks of Being a Wallflower*, directed and written by Stephen Chbosky (Santa Monica, CA: Summit Entertainment, 2012), 1:43:00, https://tv.apple.com/us/movie/the-perks-of-being-a-wallflower/umc.cmc.4xzzabee1l4dllif6xwq6e9yz.

8. *Wild*, directed by Jean-Marc Vallée, written by Nick Hornby and Cheryl Strayed (Century City, CA: Searchlight Pictures, 2014), 1:55:00, https://tv.apple.com/us/movie/wild/umc.cmc.456ppvt3rnl52v606pb73swih.

Chapter 2

1. Bob Goff, *Everybody, Always Study Guide with DVD: Becoming Love in a World Full of Setbacks and Difficult People* (Nashville, TN: Thomas Nelson, 2018).

2. Jennifer Dukes Lee, *Growing Slow: Lessons on Un-Hurrying Your Heart from an Accidental Farm Girl* (Grand Rapids, MI: Zondervan, 2021), 4.

3. "Peace Prayer," Loyola Press, accessed November 19, 2023, https://www.loyolapress.com/catholic -resources/prayer/traditional-catholic-prayers/saints-prayers/peace-prayer-of-saint-francis/.

4. *Encyclopaedia Britannica Online*, s.v. "agape," last modified September 14, 2023, https://www .britannica.com/topic/agape.

5. "Founders," No Barriers, accessed November 16, 2023, https://nobarriersusa.org/about-us /founders/.

Chapter 4

1. Pádraig Ó Tuama, *Daily Prayer with the Corrymeela Community* (London: Canterbury Press Norwich, 2017), 3.

2. Greg McKeown, "Identifying Your Circle of Competence with Kyle Westaway (Part 2)," January 19, 2023, in *The Greg McKeown Podcast*, podcast, MP3 audio, 27:28, https://podcasts.apple.com/us /podcast/163-identifying-your-circle-of-competence-with/id1513285647?i=1000595386497.

3. Jenny Odell, *How to Do Nothing: Resisting the Attention Economy* (Brooklyn, NY: Melville House, 2019), x, Kindle.

4. Annie Dillard, *The Writing Life* (New York: Harper & Row, 1989), 32.

Chapter 5

1. Maya Angelou, *Wouldn't Take Nothing for My Journey Now* (New York: Random House, 1993), 15.

2. Jack Mahoney SJ, "A Mysterious Ignatian Prayer," *Thinking Faith*, February 17, 2012, accessed November 27, 2023, https://www.thinkingfaith.org/articles/20120217_1.htm.

3. Norman MacEwan, "Norman MacEwan Quotes," Quotes.net, accessed December 26, 2023, https://www.quotes.net/authors/Norman+MacEwan.

Chapter 6

1. Desmond Tutu, "Kindness Quotes," Random Acts of Kindness Foundation, accessed December 1, 2023, https://www.randomactsofkindness.org/kindness-quotes/145-do-your-little-bit-of. Emphasis added by the author in quotation excerpts throughout the chapter.

2. "Our Story," Dressember, accessed December 23, 2023, https://www.dressember.org/story.

3. "About," The World Needs More Love Letters, accessed November 1, 2022, https://www.more loveletters.com/about.

4. Elizabeth Clemente, "Paying It Forward," *Boston College Magazine*, Fall 2022, https://www .bc.edu/content/bc-web/sites/bc-magazine/fall-2022-issue/linden-lane/pay-it-forward.html.

5. "Our Movement Makes an Impact," Dressember, accessed December 23, 2023, https://www .dressember.org/impact.

6. *Won't You Be My Neighbor?*, directed by Morgan Neville (Universal City, CA: Focus Features, 2018), 1:34:30, https://www.netflix.com/watch/80231412?source=35.

7. Becca Stevens, "#hereweare: The Beloved Community," Becca Stevens (blog), accessed November 18, 2023, https://beccastevens.org/blogs/news/hereweare-the-beloved-community.

8. Krista Tippett, "Bryan Stevenson: Finding the Courage for What's Redemptive," November 4, 2021, in *On Being with Krista Tippett*, produced by Zack Rose, Chris Heagle, and Liliana Maria Percy Ruíz, podcast, 50:46, https://onbeing.org/programs/bryan-stevenson-finding-the -courage-for-whats-redemptive/.

Chapter 7

1. Celeste Headlee, "Don't Find a Job, Find a Mission," filmed January 30, 2015, in Augusta, GA, TEDxAugusta video, 16:37, https://youtu.be/VVx6ntr5OqI?si=DqApiIFR8xpi5DkP.

2. Lisa Cron, *Story Genius: How to Use Brain Science to Go Beyond Outlining and Write a Riveting Novel (Before You Waste Three Years Writing 327 Pages That Go Nowhere)* (Berkeley, CA: Ten Speed Press, 2016), 3.

3. Headlee, "Don't Find a Job, Find a Mission."

Chapter 8

1. Aundi Kolber, "What Does It Mean to Try Softer? - Aundi Kolber," November 12, 2019, Tyndale House Publishers, YouTube video, 2:04, https://youtu.be/_KcayYEhY8U?si=YS0-oIYU0OuZhnaO.

2. John Mark Comer, *Live No Lies: Recognize and Resist the Three Enemies That Sabotage Your Peace* (Colorado Springs, CO: WaterBrook, 2021), 121.

3. E. E. Cummings, "A Poet's Advice to Students," in *A Miscellany*, First Liveright Edition (New York: Liveright, 2018), 363. Poem originally published in Ottawa Hills *Spectator*, October 26, 1955.

Chapter 9

1. Susan Cain, *Bittersweet: How Sorrow and Longing Make Us Whole* (New York: Crown, 2022), 195.

2. Francis Weller, "The Geography of Sorrow: Francis Weller on Navigating Our Losses," interview by Tim McKee, *The Sun Magazine*, October 2015, https://www.thesunmagazine.org/issues/478/the-geography-of-sorrow.

3. Paulo Coelho, *Aleph*, First Vintage International Edition (New York: Vintage Books, 2012), 266.

Chapter 10

1. Daniel Eisenberg, Sarah Ketchen Lipson, Justin Heinze, and Sasha Zhou, "The Healthy Minds Study: 2022-2023 Data Report," Healthy Minds Network, https://healthymindsnetwork.org/wp-content/uploads/2023/08/HMS_National-Report-2022-2023_full.pdf.

2. 988 Suicide and Crisis Lifeline, accessed November 27, 2023, https://988lifeline.org/.

Chapter 11

1. "Prince Rupert's Drops: 400 Year Old Mystery Revealed," May 10, 2017, Purdue Engineering, YouTube video, 2:41, https://youtu.be/lt-zvsGvtqg?si=1xUqczm-qXt-QgSA.

2. Henry David Thoreau, *Walden* (New York: Thomas Y. Crowell & Company, 1910), 11, https://www.google.com/books/edition/Walden/yiQ3AAAAIAAJ?hl=en&gbpv=1.

3. Kate Bowler, "Father Greg Boyle: The Case for Hope," February 15, 2021, in *Everything Happens with Kate Bowler*, podcast, 42:00, https://katebowler.com/podcasts/greg-boyle-the-case-for-hope/.

4. Stephen R. Covey, *The 7 Habits of Highly Effective People: Powerful Lessons in Personal Change*, 25th anniversary ed. (New York: Simon & Schuster, 2013), 88–92.

Chapter 12

1. William Shakespeare, *The Life of King Henry V,* ed. Barbara A. Mowat and Paul Werstine (Washington, DC: Folger Shakespeare Library, n.d.), accessed November 30, 2023, 4.3.2274–2277. References are to act, scene, and line. https://www.folger.edu/explore/shakespeares-works /henry-v/.

2. Shakespeare, *The Life of King Henry V,* 4.3.2296–2300.

3. Meg LeFauve and Lorien McKenna, "Andrew Stanton's Storytelling Master Class," April 11, 2021, in *The Screenwriting Life with Meg LeFauve and Lorien McKenna,* podcast, MP3 audio, 1:33:36, https:// podcasts.apple.com/us/podcast/the-screenwriting-life-with-meg-lefauve-and-lorien-mckenna /id1501641442?i=1000516654061.

Chapter 13

1. Aundi Kolber, *Try Softer: A Fresh Approach to Move Us out of Anxiety, Stress, and Survival Mode— and into a Life of Connection and Joy* (Carol Stream, IL: Tyndale Momentum, 2020), 34–35.

2. Anne Lamott, *Almost Everything: Notes on Hope* (New York: Riverhead Books, 2018), 2.

3. Lois Tonkin TTC, Cert Counselling (NZ), "Growing around Grief—Another Way of Looking at Grief and Recovery," *Bereavement Care* 15, no. 1 (Spring 1996): 10, https://doi.org/10.1080 /02682629608657376.

4. Kate Bowler, *Everything Happens for a Reason: And Others Lies I've Loved* (New York: Random House, 2019), 123.

Chapter 14

1. Hannah Brencher, "The 15-Minute Rule," *Becoming Minimalist* (blog), accessed March 20, 2023, https://www.becomingminimalist.com/15-minute-rule/.

2. Joshua J. Mark, "Tibetan Sand Mandalas," in *World History Encyclopedia,* July 15, 2021, https:// www.worldhistory.org/article/1052/tibetan-sand-mandalas/.

3. John Green, *The Anthropocene Reviewed: Essays on a Human-Centered Planet* (New York: Dutton, 2021), 106.

Chapter 15

1. Tahir Shah, *In Arabian Nights: A Caravan of Moroccan Dreams* (New York: Bantam, 2009), 138.

2. Thich Nhat Hanh, "Loving Speech & Deep Listening | Thich Nhat Hanh (short teaching video)," Plum Village App, posted on May 13, 2020, YouTube video, 9:14, https://www.you tube.com/watch?v=hDJBKEOe7Pg.

3. Chimamanda Ngozi Adichie, "The Danger of a Single Story," filmed July 2009, TEDGlobal video, 18:33, https://www.ted.com/talks/chimamanda_ngozi_adichie_the_danger_of_a_single_story.

4. John Mark Comer, "David Brooks on Politics as Secular Religion, Moral Formation & Why the Church Needs Saints Not Celebrities," September 13, 2021, in *Live No Lies Podcast,* podcast, MP3 audio, 51:25, https://podcasts.apple.com/us/podcast/david-brooks-on-politics-as -secular-religion-moral/id1585715586?i=1000535225681.

Chapter 16

1. Patrick Lencioni, *Overcoming the Five Dysfunctions of a Team: A Field Guide for Leaders, Managers, and Facilitators* (San Francisco: Jossey-Bass, 2005), 118.

2. Patrick Lencioni, *The Advantage: Why Organizational Health Trumps Everything Else in Business* (San Francisco: Jossey-Bass, 2012), 27, 37.

Chapter 17

1. C. S. Lewis, *The Weight of Glory: And Other Addresses*, 1st HarperCollins Paperback ed. (New York: HarperOne, 2001), 46.

2. John Koenig, "sonder," *The Dictionary of Obscure Sorrows* (blog), July 22, 2012, https://www.dictionaryofobscuresorrows.com/post/23536922667/sonder.

3. Walker Percy, *The Moviegoer*, First Vintage International ed. (New York: Vintage Books, 1998), 74.

Chapter 18

1. David W. Augsburger, *Caring Enough to Hear and Be Heard* (Ventura, CA: Regal Books, 1982), 12, https://openlibrary.org/books/OL3481080M/Caring_enough_to_hear_and_be_heard.

2. Sherry Turkle, *Reclaiming Conversation: The Power of Talk in a Digital Age* (New York: Penguin, 2015), 3.

3. Brené Brown, *Rising Strong: The Reckoning. The Rumble. The Revolution* (New York: Spiegel & Grau, 2015), 4.

Chapter 19

1. Kathleen Norris, *Dakota: A Spiritual Geography* (New York: Ticknor & Fields, 1993), 197.

Conclusion

1. Marina Keegan, "KEEGAN: The Opposite of Loneliness," *Yale Daily News*, May 27, 2012, https://yaledailynews.com/blog/2012/05/27/keegan-the-opposite-of-loneliness/.

2. *About Time*, directed by Richard Curtis.

ABOUT THE AUTHOR

Elizabeth McColloch is a writer and a creative with a passion for sharing meaningful stories. She encourages readers to embrace intentional living and creative generosity on her blog, Crafting a Life of Love.

Elizabeth studied business and global public health at Boston College. As a resident assistant, she drew upon her enriching college experiences to inspire her residents to live with purpose. She considers herself a "lifelong RA" and enjoys supporting other young adults with empathy and authenticity.

In her free time, Elizabeth loves connecting with friends, listening to audiobooks on long walks, and playing with her beloved goddaughter. She resides in the San Francisco Bay Area.

You can find her at

www.elizabethmccolloch.com

For additional resources, including reflection questions, visit

www.elizabethmccolloch.com/discover-what-matters-book

www.ingramcontent.com/pod-product-compliance
Lightning Source LLC
Chambersburg PA
CBHW030407130626
46549CB00004B/1665